REBEL WITH A CAUSE

Also by Monte Dutton

At Speed: *Up Close and Personal with the People, Places, and Fans of NASCAR*

REBEL WITH A CAUSE
A Season with NASCAR® Star
TONY STEWART

MONTE DUTTON

BRASSEY'S, INC.
Washington, D.C.

Library of Congress Cataloging-in-Publication Data

Dutton, Monte.
   Rebel with a cause : a season with NASCAR star Tony Stewart / Monte
Dutton.—1st ed.
       p.   cm.
   ISBN 1-57488-280-5
      1. Stewart, Tony, 1971– . 2. Automobile racing drivers—United States—
Biography. 3. NASCAR (Association)   I. Title.

GV1032.S743 D88 2001
796.72′092—dc21
[B]   2001025049

ISBN 1-57488-280-5 (alk. paper)

Printed in Canada on acid-free paper that meets the
American National Standards Institute Z39-48 Standard.

Brassey's, Inc.
22841 Quicksilver Drive
Dulles, Virginia 20166

First Edition

10 9 8 7 6 5 4 3 2 1

CONTENTS

INTRODUCTION

A REMARKABLE TALENT

Stock car racing, owing to its surge in popularity, is under constant siege from bright, talented, young drivers arriving in wave after wave to converge upon Charlotte, N.C. For those who want to go fast and make their fortune doing it, Charlotte has evolved into the promised land. In much the same fashion that actors migrate to New York and pickers to Nashville, racers descend on Charlotte and its outlying areas. The population surrounding Lake Norman, once sociologically influenced mainly by the presence of a small liberal-arts college (Davidson), is now the spiritual haven of the NASCAR culture.

The racers are everywhere. Community colleges busily design courses of study to accommodate the mechanics and find them employment. Driving schools teach the basics of driving full-bore on the NASCAR "superspeedways." Public-relations firms expand their services to cultivate the kind of refinement that will take young drivers and make them "sponsor-friendly." Teeth are fixed, vision corrected, accents softened, and wardrobes upgraded: Henry Higgins would be envious.

Remarkably unaffected by all these contrivances is a young man from Indiana named Tony Stewart.

While all around him gurus and charlatans are busily attempting to clone Jeff Gordon, Stewart is just as forcefully resisting those who want to turn him into someone he isn't. As such, Stewart is the only potential folk hero in a sport that used to be characterized by them.

Fireball Roberts and Curtis Turner are dead, Richard Petty and Junior Johnson retired. The beginning of the 2001 season saw the circuit lose perhaps its greatest folk hero ever when Dale Earnhardt was killed in a crash on the last lap of the Daytona 500.

Stewart is the only young dinosaur still tramping the forest.

Nonbelievers observing Stewart predict he will change. Railbirds nod knowingly and say things like, "I remember when (insert driver name) was just like that."

But few race-car drivers have ever been as resistant to change and as stubborn as the 29-year-old Stewart. Stewart, who grew up in the Indiana towns of Columbus and Rushville, believes success is worthless unless it can be experienced on its own—no, his own—terms. His absolute commitment to preserving his distinct identity is a constant source of conflict between Stewart and those around him.

Once, in 1999, when Stewart had been recruited to endorse a line of Nike footwear earmarked for the race-car crowd, a company spokesman sent a script for Stewart to recite at the press conference concocted for the occasion. Stewart wadded it up and tossed it into the trash.

"No way," he said. "I'm not going to read any script. I know what they want, and I'm damn well capable of putting it in my own words."

As mercurial as this bright young Roman candle can be, Stewart is widely admired for his roguish independence. Even the driver's perpetually fretting personal assistant, Judy Kouba Dominick, loves Stewart for the very qualities that keep her nervous.

That Stewart is different has not been lost on the fans. After only one season on the Winston Cup circuit—the most successful rookie season in stock car racing history—an astonishing number of fans were already following Stewart's every move. The decision of Atlanta-based retailer Home Depot to sponsor Stewart's racing efforts has turned into one of the more fortuitous moves in recent advertising history. The names Tony Stewart and Home Depot have become entwined to an extent the retailer could not possibly have envisioned.

Tony Stewart has already won championships in bodies as diverse as the Indy Racing League, United States Auto Club, and International Karting Federation, but never in his young career had he captured the imagination of race fans as he did in 1999, when he became the highest-finishing rookie in the NASCAR point standings in 33 years. Stewart's three victories were the most ever by a first-year driver.

On the occasion of his eighth start, Stewart qualified first. His first top-10 finish occurred at the series' most demanding track, Darlington Raceway in South Carolina. Stewart won his 25th race.

The most successful driver of the 1990s, Jeff Gordon, said he thought Stewart might have more talent than anyone he'd ever seen. The declaration was particularly noteworthy since many experts would say the same about Gordon.

For all of Gordon's virtuosity, though, he and Stewart are peers, virtually the same age and both products of Indiana (Gordon was born in California but moved to the Midwest in his early teens). The NASCAR figure who fascinated Stewart was Dale Earnhardt, with whom he raced for two years before Earnhardt's untimely death in early 2001.

When Stewart's romantic bid to win both the Indianapolis 500 and the Coca-Cola 600 (at Lowe's Motor Speedway in Concord, North Carolina) ended in exhaustion (and a fourth-place finish), it was Earnhardt who appeared from nowhere to offer some good-natured ribbing when Stewart was being spirited to the infield first-aid center.

"That's the way he is," Stewart recalled. "Every time I see him, every time I talk to him, it's like he comes out of thin air. He cracks a joke, laughs at me, and then he's gone." Stewart was silent for a moment. "You know, I like that guy."

At the gas pumps that night after the completion of his 1,100-mile odyssey, Stewart had somehow managed to pull himself from his car without assistance. When he tried to walk, however, his legs gave out, and the resulting swoon drew shrieks from the gathering post-race crowd. As the young driver was hoisted back to his feet, his arms draped around the shoulders of others, Earnhardt swooped in to say something along the lines of, "Well, rookie, you had enough racing for one night?"

Stewart, who barely even remembered the race's final 100 miles, somehow recalled every detail of Earnhardt's brief appearance in his field of vision.

"He's been good to me," Stewart said of the seven-time champion. "It's been kind of fun with him. Even in some practices, he has kind of raced me harder than he did in the races. He's never laid a bumper or fender to me, and he has raced me clean all year. He's been the most fun guy to race this year.

"I can remember the first race. We pitted side by side, and I was nervous thinking this guy was going to growl and snarl and give me dirty looks. One time I was climbing in my car, and he'd pull out. One time I was leaning on my toolbox, and he'd kick my legs out, just joking around. He was always a guy I looked up to when I watched Winston Cup on TV, and it's been neat to interact with him."

Where Stewart goes, action follows. He is as colorful off the track as he is talented on it. In an age where many Winston Cup drivers are surrounded—some say suffocated—by public-relations operatives and assorted handlers, Stewart is unconquerable.

"I am what I am; take me or leave me," Stewart said. "If you don't like what you get, shop around the garage, and there are 50 other guys, and you can find what you're looking for. I always get in trouble when I lose, whether I blow an engine or get crashed or whatever, and that's when I stick my foot in my mouth. Then everybody seems to be like a vulture flying over my head."

It is important to Stewart that he be his own man, and that means resisting those who would script his every move.

Stewart drives race cars. It is all he wants to do. He is obsessed by them. The single most surprising aspect of his personality is his relentless ability to concentrate solely on racing. He is obviously intelligent. His sense of humor is well developed. Yet the farther he drifts from the unruly clatter of the racetrack, the more discontented he becomes.

He shies away from mobs, becoming irritable when roving bands of fans overrun him in search of garage-area autographs and when reporters stick microphones and tape recorders in his face. Yet he spends as many hours signing autographs, usually in the "souvenir cities" surrounding tracks, as anyone. While Stewart's fuse can be short, almost none of the journalists who regularly cover the sport say they have anything but admiration for him. The general consensus in the press is that Stewart's spontaneity and honesty are worth making allowances for his unpredictable nature.

"Talk to my crew guys and people that see me away from the racetrack, and 90 percent of the time I'm totally different than I am at the racetrack," Stewart said. "It gets disappointing because you have to mold yourself to what people want you to be. That's been the great thing about Home Depot, Pontiac, and [owner] Joe Gibbs, because they have let me be me."

Whatever quality it is that Stewart possesses, whatever the lightly sketched lines that define his charisma, fans react. Before the October 1999 race at Lowe's Motor Speedway, a Charlotte radio/TV personality offered the matter-of-fact opinion that Stewart's qualifying run had been greeted by a greater roar than either Earnhardt's or Gordon's.

"I had no clue it would be this way," said Stewart. "It's been the best part of it. When you go out and get that kind of reception at driver introductions, it's worth a 10th of a second each lap for the rest of the day. It's neat to have that kind of support. Unless you grew up in the South, it's usually hard to get the fan support. They have welcomed me with open arms."

Stewart should, by all rights, be a pariah in an age dominated by the "Stepford drivers" who equate success with making all the right moves off the track. Many of Stewart's colleagues, especially the young ones, are all too willing to have their every public appearance scripted, choreographed, and molded.

In contrast, Stewart's actions practically scream out: Can a man who's sold his soul off the track keep his soul on it?

"If I accepted losing, why would you want me to drive your race car?" he said. "There are times I get sick of being politically correct. I got into Winston Cup because I wanted to be a race-car driver. If I wanted to be a politician, I would be in Washington."

Stewart was asked if he had ever heard the French term *enfant terrible*. His expression said that they had not taught much French at the dirt tracks of his native Indiana. Told a loose translation of the term would be "bad boy," Stewart smiled and said, "Hey, maybe I ought to paint that on my crash helmet."

Despite the occasional eruptions, Stewart is also unfailingly modest. When honors are heaped upon him, his voice can be no more imposing than that of a schoolboy. When properly calmed, he is even willing to poke fun at himself.

Oh, yes. Most of the time he admits his mistakes, albeit grudgingly.

After the now-famous 1999 Martinsville, Virginia, incident in which he and Kenny Irwin feuded, Stewart was fined $5,000 for "conduct detrimental to the sport." The two drivers, rivals on the open-wheel circuits of their native Indiana long before they moved south to race stock cars, had engaged in a "beating and banging" session that ended with Stewart's Pontiac being shoved into the turn-one wall. After Stewart had climbed out of his smoking heap, glaring murderously, he fired a pair of heat shields at the windshield of Irwin's Ford as Irwin drove past on the succeeding yellow-flag lap. When Irwin slowed for what one suspects was a quick gesture or profanity, Stewart dove somewhat tentatively through the passenger-side window, flailing away with some sort of futile southpaw jab and then bounding back out of the enemy vehicle as Irwin sped away.

"I felt stupid," Stewart said later. "One thing about me, I take everything that happens with auto racing, as far as my career, I take it very seriously. If I didn't care about anything that goes on, you wouldn't see me react at all. I care very passionately about what I do as a race-car driver. That's why I got as angry as I did, and that's how I acted."

Yet this self-proclaimed shame did not prevent Stewart from defending himself against the sport's thought police.

"I probably got 175 e-mails from people complaining about how bad I was, and this and that," he added. "Everybody that sits at home and watches it on TV, they need to come out here and do this. I guarantee you it's a higher-stress job than what most people have. We're not machines. We're not robots. I can't be a perfect person every time. I'm going to make mistakes. If people can't accept me making mistakes, I can't do anything about it.

"I'm going to do the best I can to make up for what I've done. I'm sorry for what I did. At the same time, in the heat of battle, you're going to do things that aren't right, and you're going to do things you regret. There's nothing you can do about it but go on. Hopefully, everybody can let it go and let us go back to racing. They need to have some kind of passion in this sport. If there weren't, the races would be boring, and nobody would want to watch them to begin with. Our personalities inside the car, whether we're having a good day or a bad day, it's the personalities that make this sport, anyway."

NASCAR was unimpressed with Stewart's antics, but most of the crowd of 80,000 was. Those who monitor such things quickly reported, in the days following the incident, a huge upsurge in Stewart's fan-club membership and T-shirt sales.

Has this *wunderkind* been accepted by veterans who have found less acclaim in a decade than Stewart received that one tawdry afternoon?

Four days after the Martinsville incident, a group presented Stewart with a wad of greenbacks, kicking off a fund to pay his fine. The group in question was Kenny Irwin's pit crew.

"I was really surprised at the beginning of the season," he said. "Nobody was really rough with me at the beginning of the year. You had guys that were testing you a little bit, but nobody was really roughing me up and taking me out. I thought the first half of the season was going to be really rough. It's hard to pick a point in the season where I think things changed because everything went so smoothly at the beginning of the year, and everybody treated me so nice and was so open with information, there really wasn't a transformation.

"I never really thought about if I belonged. I felt if Joe Gibbs (the former Washington Redskins coach who is Stewart's car owner) believed in me and (teammate) Bobby Labonte believed in me, then I belonged because they felt like I belonged, so I really didn't think about that aspect. But I was surprised how they accepted and how well they treated me at the beginning of the season."

Stewart's life was always a whirlwind, but the demands of his mushrooming celebrity sometimes trouble him. Like every driver, he has promotional obligations with his various sponsors. He co-owns Indy Racing League and USAC Silver Crown teams. A typical weekday night may find him testing his Cup car, watching his 63-year-old father race TQ (three-quarter) midget cars, racing his own dirt Late Model, or just sitting in the grandstands at some modest local track. No level of racing is beneath Stewart; if he concludes that he has even an hour to spare, he will charge off in a rental car just to find a track and watch the races. Twice during his rookie season, at Pocono Raceway in Pennsylvania, Stewart and crew chief Greg Zipadelli searched in vain for an elusive quarter-midget track where, theoretically, they could have watched youngsters competing on a ⅛-mile postage stamp of dirt.

To Stewart, racing is a business, a profession, a hobby, and a spectator sport, all rolled into one.

Once acquainted with Stewart, the observer discovers a painstaking honesty and a personality fraught with contradictions. By his own admission, he is a different person when he is strapped into a race car. Outside the cockpit, the humility is genuine. When he insists that all the success has taken him by surprise, he means it. But no one who watches him drive or who monitors the radio conversations between him and his crew would call Stewart modest.

At the ¾-mile track in Richmond, Virginia, the site of his first victory, Stewart seemed supremely confident, reassuring his own crew when pit stops caused his track position to suffer.

"Don't worry, guys," he said. "They're not going anywhere."

If the rookie season had not been so magical, if Stewart had not managed to win even one race, let alone three, the ride would have been just as rewarding, Stewart said. "I wouldn't have looked back and regretted any of it," he said. "Like I said, we always talk about how competitive the series is. I never expected to win a race. . . . It's a luxury to win. Like I've said before, it's like a dream come true for me to be involved in this series. It's been more than I dreamed could have happened in a rookie season.

"It's not because of Tony Stewart. . . . It's definitely a team effort. I was a rookie in Winston Cup, but I wasn't a rookie in racing. I've been racing 20 years, and I know what it takes to win races with race teams and how that chemistry has to be there and the team has to jell. From day one, this race team, we came out of the box, and we acted like we'd worked with each other all our lives. We never felt like we had to learn each other. We all just got into the deal and acted like we'd known each other all our lives."

Stewart had been NASCAR's best rookie ever, a claim that was hardly even disputed. He had been the first rookie to win as many as three races, the first to win even one race in 12 years, and the first to finish as high as fourth in the Cup points race in 33 years. To some extent, his success even outshone the championship season of veteran Dale Jarrett.

In 1980, another driver, one with the last name Earnhardt, had won the Winston Cup championship one year after being named its best rookie. As the 2000 season dawned, many were watching closely to see if Stewart could duplicate that feat.

What followed was equal parts ordeal and triumph. By year's end, the difficulty of winning a championship had been thoroughly impressed on Stewart and his fans. Stewart had also proved that his rookie season was no fluke, and that there was almost no limit to his potential.

Seldom were there dull moments.

HE CAN BE A MEDIA DARLING

TREVOSE, Pennsylvania
January 2000

Tony Stewart breezed into a banquet room at the Radisson Hotel and instantly became the center of attention. About 200 journalists, all members of the Eastern Motorsports Press Association (EMPA), had been impressed enough by Stewart's rookie season in the NASCAR Winston Cup Series to award him their Al Holbert Memorial Award as the organization's driver of the year. It was quite an unexpected honor since Stewart had been selected over Dale Jarrett, the Winston Cup champion; Juan Montoya, who had dominated the CART champ-car circuit; and John Force, the champion of the National Hot Rod Association's Funny Car classification.

The 28-year-old Hoosier immediately charmed the audience as he answered their questions from the dais. He was modest and seemed genuinely moved by the honor. Though not an Easterner himself, Stewart played to the audience's populist sensibilities.

Unlike in the South, where stock car racing is king, the East is home to many other forms of automobile racing. Many of the writers and photographers present had spent the previous year tramping around the dirt tracks where Stewart still felt at home. When one of them asked Stewart where he would be racing in a perfect world, one in which money did not matter, he replied almost immediately. "I guess I'd still be racing sprints and midgets on some dirt track."

It was what they wanted him to say, but it was also the truth.

Stewart had captured the imagination of the EMPA because they saw him as a glorious throwback to a bygone age when giants like A.J. Foyt and Mario Andretti had cheerfully stepped into and out of wildly different forms of race cars on an almost daily basis. The EMPA members had begun paying attention as Stewart developed a cult follow-ing in his native Midwest. Now he had arrived in what had become the country's favorite form of motorsports, stock car racing, but without losing touch with his rough-and-tumble past.

Playfully Stewart confirmed the romantic suspicions of his audience. When asked a question about his lingering "extracurricular activities" at short tracks, Stewart prefaced his answer by saying, "Now, first, guys, is this going to appear in any publication that Joe Gibbs (his Winston Cup car owner) might see?"

Another reporter noted that Stewart had emerged uninjured from a wintertime tumble in an open-wheel midget he'd been racing on an indoor track.

"Yeah, Joe (Gibbs) asked me about that," Stewart said, drawing conspiratorial chuckles. "I told him, 'Well, y'know, Coach, the track was so small that you could just about run around the thing as fast as you were driving it.' And he said, 'Well, if you were going so slow, wonder how come you turned upside-down?'"

When asked about a technical matter related to NASCAR, Stewart said, "Heck, I don't know. You know me. I ain't been paying attention." Then he called out to a veteran NASCAR reporter in the audience and asked him to answer the question. The reporter blushed, nonetheless appreciative of Stewart referring to him by name in front of a room full of colleagues.

It doesn't take long to recognize Stewart's intelligence, but he has not always been so charming. Six months before the EMPA banquet, he had stalked out of the garage area without a word, having run out of fuel in a race he would have won had he stopped to replenish his supply. The New England press corps had been furious at Stewart that day, but a few of them were in the audience at the EMPA convention, and clearly time had healed the rift.

He is a hard person to dislike for any length of time, this Stewart. Why? Because in a world dominated by those who tilt their heads to their handlers, Stewart remains his own man. What one sees is what one gets. He is never afraid to be Tony.

But even for a man with such a clear sense of himself, breaking into NASCAR can be difficult. "That's the part that I'm learning," Stewart said after the banquet. "You hear people talk about how tough the rookie season is. I'm finding out that's not all out on the racetrack. There's a lot of adjusting to be done, you know, learning how to get in and out of racetracks, just there's so many new things to learn. You learn to fight for the things that are important to you. It's an adjustment that hasn't all occurred yet. We got a good start on it [last] year. By the end of [this] year, we'll have a pretty good handle on it."

What eventually earns Stewart the admiration of reporters—at least those who see him regularly—is his utter candor. Some wonder how long he can maintain it in the face of his booming popularity.

"Every time I go in the media center, people say don't change," Stewart said. "Why be the same as everybody else? If I wanted to be the same as everybody else, I'd be wearing (three-time Winston Cup champion) Jeff Gordon's clothes to the racetrack, I'd walk around like Jeff, I'd do what Jeff does. I'm my own person, this is what I am, and take me or leave me. You've got to be politically correct at times, but it's nice to be able to express what you believe, what you think, at times. I've been a firm believer, if a guy asks you an honest question, you give him an honest answer. It may not be what the guy wants to hear, but I think people respect that.

"Sometimes it does get me in trouble, but do the people want to hear 'no comment'? No. They want to hear the answer to the question. You can't keep people happy and be yourself both, or at least you can't do it all the time, or at least I can't. I don't try to please everybody all the time. If somebody asks me a question, I'm going to give him an honest answer."

Is it any wonder he won the award?

2

A DISASTROUS BEGINNING

DAYTONA BEACH, Florida
February 2000

Tony Stewart does not like Daytona International Speedway or, rather, the form racing takes on the track's high banks. Stewart prefers self-reliance, and Daytona requires teamwork. Not that Stewart is averse to being the willing partner on occasion: his cooperative efforts with teammate Bobby Labonte are the foundation upon which Joe Gibbs Racing is built. A man ought to win the Daytona 500 on his own merits and those of his car, though. This business of needing help in order to pass anybody is for the birds.

For safety reasons, two NASCAR tracks, Daytona and Talladega (Alabama) Superspeedway, require that "restrictor plates" be placed between each car's carburetor and intake manifold to limit horsepower, thus reducing the speeds which may be attained. These plates make it nearly impossible for a lone car to gather enough speed to pass another, so the drivers group together in "drafts." The air shooting over the top of the front car envelopes those behind it, creating a situation in which the cars travel faster in groups than by zipping around the high-banked tracks alone. Under such circumstances, for one car to pull out of line and move forward in the draft, the driver must work in unison with at least one other competitor.

Routinely, Daytona (and Talladega) racing involves teamwork and betrayal as drivers send signals to one another by hand. When a driver moves out to pass and finds no one to help him, he's been "hung out to dry." Inevitably, his car is passed by the entire line from which he just broke rank.

Notwithstanding the frustrations of racing at Daytona International Speedway, Stewart arrived in Daytona Beach in a wonderful mood, rested and ready to embark on another season. One key to his good humor lay 40 miles away. The phalanx of mechanics, marketers, flacks, and souvenir sellers assembled by Joe Gibbs Racing did not constitute Stewart's only team.

At Volusia County Speedway, located inland at Barberville, Stewart had assembled a chest of play toys that would have boggled the mind of Richie Rich. In addition to offering a dizzying array of events encompassing almost a month at the 2.5-mile superspeedway, Daytona's Speedweeks draws short trackers from all over the country—particularly those whose activities have been curtailed by ill weather—to compete at nearby tracks like Volusia County, New Smyrna, East Bay, and St. Augustine. Stewart had cheerfully overscheduled himself, a habit of his. He'd arranged for his own Late Model, sponsored by the chain of J.D. Byrider used-car lots, to be towed down from Indiana. Brett Hearn had brought an "experimental" dirt modified from Pennsylvania for Stewart to try. Danny Lasoski had arrived to race the winged sprint car that Stewart owns.

What enabled Stewart to load himself with extracurricular activities was, tacitly, the attitude of Winston Cup team owner (and former Hall of Fame football coach) Joe Gibbs, who possesses keen intuition and a remarkably enlightened understanding of what makes young competitors tick. Perhaps Gibbs knew that, in due course, the headstrong

Stewart would learn for himself the perils of an overbooked schedule. Perhaps Gibbs was just too preoccupied; he'd spent much of Speedweeks at the bedside of his ill mother. For whatever reason, Daytona turned into a nightmarish ordeal for Stewart, who soon found trouble in his professional paradise.

A racer has to race. That was Stewart's motto when he arrived in Daytona. He thought he could manage all his commitments, just as he had thought himself up to the task of racing 1,100 miles in one 24-hour period the previous May. After running Indy and then flying to Charlotte to compete in the Coca-Cola 600 on the same day, an exhausted Stewart had reluctantly concluded that the strain was too much. Deep down, Stewart knew the quixotic doubleheader had probably cost him his first Winston Cup victory. He had finished fourth in the Coke 600, but, at race's end, he had collapsed in the garage area. No one had ever completed both races before, although two drivers, John Andretti and Robby Gordon, had tried.

"I could've won the 600 if I'd been physically strong at the end of the race," Stewart had admitted.

The decision to curtail his Indy Racing League activities had been Stewart's own, however. Gibbs had watched carefully, no doubt fretting over the well-being of the brilliant young driver.

"He doesn't necessarily say a lot," said Stewart of Gibbs. "He just gives you that coach's look."

"Whenever we have decisions to make, we all get together," said Gibbs. "As far as racing these cars is concerned, I'm not the expert. It doesn't matter what you do in life, whether it's coaching football or racing cars, you have to put good people in place and let them do their jobs. I try to spend my time working in areas where I can help the team."

Once again, at Daytona, the lessons would be hard.

After the Bud Shootout, the annual all-star race reserved for pole winners from the previous season, Stewart climbed out of his car baffled, despite a respectable fourth-place finish.

"Aw, I'm just frustrated," he said. "I was upset that Bobby (Labonte, his teammate) got wrecked. That, plus I don't know what I'm doing out there."

Stewart was exaggerating, of course, but it was an interesting statement from a driver who had been recently touted as the most successful rookie in NASCAR history. He was not referring to actual driving ability, but rather the nuances—the high-speed chess, if you will—required for success in the Daytona draft. Experience is a powerful factor. A driver has to learn the aerodynamic intricacies of how cars behave in close proximity to one another: he must know whether to line up with others on the outside or inside, how not to be caught unawares when other cars shift one way or the other, how the massive lines of cars are moving relative to one another.

It requires much more than a mere seat-of-the-pants knack for driving a single car fast around a closed course. Drafting requires patience, and Stewart would be the first to admit that patience is not one of his more notable virtues.

"I'm serious," he said. "I just get tired of relying on everybody else to help you out. It takes a lot of knowledge to know when to go and when to stay put. I feel like I'm holding up the rest of the team at this track."

"He (Stewart) is just right there with the rest of us," said Jeff Gordon, smiling, when informed of Stewart's remarks. "It takes time to get the hang of it."

Later, following a midweek practice session, Stewart engaged in a brief altercation with rival driver Robby Gordon (unrelated to Jeff).

Gordon, an ex-open-wheeler like Stewart, lost control of his Ford after it bumped against Stewart's Pontiac. Gordon, making a return to NASCAR with a new team he had formed with two partners, stormed angrily into the garage enclave occupied by Stewart's team. After Stewart climbed out of his car, the two confronted each other, a small shoving match ensued, and Stewart's crewmen pulled Gordon away from their driver. One team member, Jason Shapiro, received a stiff fine ($2,000) from NASCAR because the governing body found his peacemaking tactics a bit too harsh. Apparently, a video account of the incident— the garage area, as usual, being full of roaming television crews— revealed that, in pulling Gordon away from Stewart, Shapiro had shoved Gordon either to the ground or against a hard object. Gordon was uninjured, thankfully.

Stewart himself escaped NASCAR's formal wrath, and he and Gordon quickly patched up their differences. Gordon visited Stewart in his motor coach later that day, prompting Stewart to say, "I thought it was awfully big of Robby to come over and get it straightened out. There's no lingering bad will."

Far more anguishing were Stewart's experiences at Volusia County Speedway, the dirt track located nearly an hour's drive from the Winston Cup venue.

Few people know that Stewart becomes claustrophobic in crowds. An intrusive influx of humanity often causes him to become panicky and, occasionally, almost hysterical. He also insists on privacy when he is working on his race cars, an insistence that sometimes creates a bad impression among the fans, who roam garage areas en masse during practice sessions. Stewart regularly ventures outside tracks to sign autographs at the transporters where his souvenirs are sold, and his schedule is crowded with personal appearances. Apart from required activities, though, Stewart's affection for his fans is genuine. He insists, however, on wholly separating his fan activities from his racing activities. The combination of this policy, his claustrophobia, and often overzealous fans creates embarrassing scenes from time to time. To help manage the situation, Stewart often retains security officers to keep fans away from him.

At the dirt track, Stewart was so harried by fans and television crews during a stint driving his Late Model that he declared that he was no longer going to sign any autographs or submit to interviews.

When photographers continued to mill around near his car's pit stall, Stewart became angry. At least one relatively innocent bystander felt the wrath of Stewart's verbal abuse, for which the driver later apologized personally. A local television reporter tried unsuccessfully to interview Stewart and, after another angry scene, vilified Stewart on the 11 o'clock news.

"I can't win," Stewart said the following morning. "No matter what I do, they're going to make me out to be a jerk. I think I'd better stop driving on the short tracks and just concentrate on being a car owner."

Stewart promised to fulfill obligations he had already made to race in several short-track contests, but, clearly, the price of his sudden rise in popularity was becoming too great a burden. His moonlighting was encroaching increasingly on his Winston Cup stardom. Actually, it would be more accurate to say that stardom was encroaching on Stewart's ability to live a happy, uninterrupted life.

Before Daytona, Stewart had gone to Avondale, Arizona, ostensibly to serve as grand marshal for the Copper World Classic, the annual winter speed festival held at Phoenix International Raceway. Once in the desert, Stewart's plans suddenly changed. He wound up competing in three separate races, winning one and qualifying fastest for another. Volusia, however, proved more trying.

When NASCAR hotshots compete on local tracks, the action can be fierce. Local drivers who will never advance to higher levels put special effort into their rare races against the celebrities. Once upon a time, appearances like the one Stewart made at Volusia County were more common. Legends like Harry Gant and Bobby Allison often took part in match races against each other and against the local heroes, but the huge growth of the sport in the 1990s mostly put an end to such spectacles. Before Stewart arrived on the scene, Ken Schrader had been the only remaining Winston Cup driver who occasionally competed on the small-town "bull rings."

Stewart could easily have shown up at short tracks strictly to sign autographs, earning handsome pay in the process, but what brought him to Volusia County Speedway was racing. If he paid no attention to the actual races and acceded to the mobs brazenly demanding his time, he would have put himself at higher risk for a catastrophic accident. He would also have made winning less likely. To Stewart, winning is the reason one becomes a racer.

After once again finding himself exasperated at the crush of the autograph hounds, the fans popping their flashbulbs and asking him to pose, sign their T-shirts, kiss their babies, and sign their trading cards, finally Stewart saw what those around him had been predicting. It was too much. He had to meet with his mechanics. He had to "groove" his tires and decide how many pounds of air to pump into them. Dirt-track racing is a much more complicated art than most people realize, and the decisions Stewart had to make were ones that might have made the difference between sliding under a checkered flag and flipping down a back stretch.

Stewart refused further autograph requests and declined interviews. Fans booed him, cursed him, and called him ungrateful. The television crew shoved a microphone in his face, and he told them where to stick it. By the following morning, unflattering accounts of the incident had made the rounds of the superspeedway. The fans wanted Stewart to run the short tracks, but they wouldn't give him the common courtesies accorded every other driver in the infield. The other drivers spent their time trying to figure out a way to beat Tony Stewart, but Stewart was essentially being asked to ignore his race car and cater to every whim of the press and his fans.

Stewart awoke that morning in his motor coach—parked in the Daytona infield—numbed by the disquieting events of the previous night. It was then that he made the inevitable decision to put a stop to the madness.

"I'm sick of it," Stewart said. "That's it. They make me out to be a jerk no matter what I do. I sign a hundred autographs and the one guy left out spits at me. I do a hundred interviews, and finally try to do what I'm supposed to do, which is try to get my car running good, and I'm all over the TV as an ungrateful jackass. I don't enjoy making people mad, believe me. It's just gotten to the point where there's no way out."

The decision to phase himself out of the short-track business was difficult, simply because it was a pastime he enjoyed more than anything else in his life. He decided to confine his duties to that of a car owner ("For some reason, people leave me alone when I'm just hanging out trying to help somebody else," he said) and devote all his other time to the many responsibilities related to his Winston Cup career.

"I'm going to fulfill the commitments I've already made, and that's it," Stewart said. "It's the only solution, and I hate it's come to this."

So the last of the old-fashioned racers, the last of a line descended from Tiny Lund, Little Bud Moore, and Schrader, decided to knuckle under. In theory, everyone had loved him for being a throwback, but as a practical matter, the same people had taken all the fun out of it.

Race fans like to tell stories of watching contemporary stars "back where it all started." Most tell rueful tales of how time changed their heroes. Yet the majority of Stewart's problems stem from his unwillingness to be changed by time and fame.

No, the big stars don't run short tracks anymore. They don't mingle with the average Joe. They lose touch with their roots.

Wonder why?

Ultimately, Stewart's decision to give up the short tracks was not a permanent one. Short-track racing, stripped of the trappings of stardom, is a valuable therapy for Stewart, who had occasionally shown up at local dirt tracks like 311 Speedway in Madison, North Carolina (near the Winston Cup track in Martinsville, Virginia), just to sit anonymously in the stands and watch the action. In most instances, Stewart's little avocation allows him to escape, however briefly, the glare of public scrutiny. The Daytona Beach area, already crowded with NASCAR fans, turned out to be an exception.

At the time Stewart said he was giving up short-track racing, he probably meant it. He had, no doubt, been counseled to concentrate on his Winston Cup career and perhaps even to spend more of his time attending to business interests. To Stewart, though, Cup racing is almost a job, while the short tracks are his hobby. He races the dirt tracks primarily out of his love for the sport.

Within a couple of months, though, he was back out in the sticks, racing occasionally at the quarter-mile, lightly banked oval at the Jackson County Fairgrounds in Brownstown, Indiana. In the end, what Stewart probably learned was that he simply had to avoid competing at small tracks located near the NASCAR venues.

Stewart is excitable, emotional, moody, clever, even snide, but it would be a stretch to label him a spoiled brat. He is a racer from a simpler age, one in which it was much easier to be versatile. In October 1999, Stewart had spent a glorious weekend racing for millions of dollars on the Winston Cup Series at Talladega Superspeedway and for hundreds of dollars at Talladega Short Track, just up the street. Observers noted that he had been happier, and more in his element, at the dirt track. Even there, though, he had experienced problems when some fans attended the short-track proceedings to seek him out for autographs and photos instead of to watch him race.

The Daytona 500, NASCAR's biggest race, wound up being another disappointment. Stewart performed well in his 125-mile qualifying race, held on the Sunday prior to the official Winston Cup season opener, finishing fourth.

"We were best in class," he said afterward, obviously in reference to the Ford superiority that permeated the entire Daytona experience. "I'm pretty happy. The car was a lot better than it was two days ago. The guys did a great job. Greg (Zipadelli) and all the guys really turned this car around. It's a whole different race car than what we had.

"The Pontiac has been good everywhere we've gone, and I think right now we're just getting 'snookered' a little bit. The car is driving really well. We're just getting beat. We're just getting outrun right now."

Realistically, and prophetically, Stewart said he did not think he could win the 500, however.

"Not at the rate we are right now," he opined. "We can run with the pack. We just can't run with those guys that ran up front. We've got our work cut out to get it ready for Sunday. I ran with a Ford all day and can't say that nobody is going to run with us, because there were two Chevys behind us and then another Pontiac. Right now, we just have to do our work and try to catch up to where they are. I was about two tenths (of a second) off what the front three guys (Bill Elliott, Dale Jarrett, Rusty Wallace, all in Fords) were running while I was leading [the second] pack, so we have to find two tenths somewhere."

The two tenths he never found. Jarrett won the season's opening race, which was described in many a newspaper account as the dullest running of the so-called "Great American Race" in years. The contest featured the fewest lead changes in 35 years.

Stewart also suffered one more bit of ill fortune in the race. A pit-road accident injured one of his crewmen, and it could have been much worse. Teammate Bobby Labonte's Grand Prix pitted directly in front of Stewart's. On three consecutive pit stops, the right-rear tire from Labonte's Pontiac squirted away from the tire carrier when removed from the car. Each time Stewart's car was right behind Labonte's, and twice the escaped tire had devastating consequences for Stewart and his team. Once Stewart ran directly into the loose tire as he pulled out, shoving it two thirds of the way down pit road in what looked like some ungainly new form of shuffleboard. The dent in Stewart's front air dam required massive repair and was largely responsible for his 17th-place finish.

The second incident was almost tragic. Just as Stewart was receiving radio communication that pit work had been completed, one of his crewmen, Mike Lingerfelt, spotted yet another loose Labonte tire. Lingerfelt scrambled to retrieve the tire just as Stewart was peeling out of the pit stall. Stewart's car hit Lingerfelt as the crewman was bringing the loose tire under control, instantly snapping the bone in Lingerfelt's thigh. Perhaps out of instinct, or maybe just luck, Lingerfelt had managed to cushion the blow by placing the tire between his body and the onrushing car.

Lingerfelt required surgery at Daytona Beach's Halifax Medical Center on the day after the race and faced a lengthy recovery process.

Stewart remained as frustrated by the nuances of drafting as he had been by the annoyances of his short-track activities. He still managed to improve on the previous year's performance, when he had finished 28th in his first visit to NASCAR's most prestigious race. Nonetheless, it was a difficult start to his sophomore season in the country's most popular motorsports series.

3

BACK TO NORMAL

ROCKINGHAM, North Carolina
February 2000

The transition from Daytona to North Carolina Speedway is a stark one.

The Daytona 500 is the most prestigious of all NASCAR races, held at its most famous venue. Rockingham is a quaint little mile (actually 1.017 mile) with a seating capacity of about 60,000—minute by contemporary standards. As such, the track's very survival is in question, particularly its status as one of the 13 tracks that host two NASCAR events each year.

Rockingham's future seemed even more in question when, on a cold, overcast Sunday afternoon in the Carolina sand hills, an unexpectedly small crowd of 45,000 showed up for the Dura-Lube/Kmart 400. The race's television ratings were also a disappointment, down 16 percent from the previous year.

Located in a sparsely populated area, its fan base crowded by nearby tracks in Concord, North Carolina, and Darlington, South Carolina, North Carolina Speedway is precisely the kind of place stock car racing may eventually outgrow. This is a shame. For one thing, the track's small size and elevated grandstands give it the best sight lines on the entire circuit. It is also a challenging track that rewards driver skill in ways that the newer cookie-cutter tracks—all wider, similarly shaped, and less banked—do not. Its abrasive pavement also rewards drivers who have a knack for minimizing tire wear.

Tony Stewart very nearly won a Busch Grand National race at Rockingham in 1998, losing by half a car length to Matt Kenseth. It was the closest Stewart ever came to a victory in NASCAR's version of the Triple-A minor leagues. In his first Cup race at Rockingham, on February 21, 1999, he finished 11th.

Stewart looked fondly to Rockingham, anxious to put the misfortune and turmoil of Daytona behind him.

"I was just glad to get out of Daytona," Stewart said later. "When you look at everything that happened, Daytona was almost a nightmare. My feeling when I got to Rockingham was basically relief that we were getting back to 'real racing.' "

The small crowd enjoyed racing that was vastly superior to the Daytona 500 the previous week. The middle stages were breathtakingly contested, but the end evolved into a fascinating, more subtle game between Stewart's teammate, Bobby Labonte, and the aging veteran Dale Earnhardt.

Daytona is one kind of chess game; Rockingham is quite another. Daytona is a high-speed game of strategy, easy by no stretch of the imagination, but different from tracks with less steep banks. The advantage enjoyed at Daytona by an Earnhardt, or three-time winner Dale Jarrett, is one of experience at handling deftly the problem-solving of the draft. Since engines are hindered by the restrictor plates clamped onto the carburetors, cars circling Daytona's 2.5 miles are slowed by perhaps 20 mph. Cooperation between drivers, and frequent betrayal of one by another, are the hallmarks of a typical Daytona race.

The winner at Rockingham must have a knack for wrestling a

3,400-pound car around and around at the highest speeds possible but without wearing out the all-important rubber. Stewart possesses such a knack, but impetuosity got the best of him at the end.

After starting 15th, Stewart fell a lap behind during the race's first hundred miles. As almost always seems to be the case, however, he and his crew worked patiently to make up the disadvantage. Greg Zipadelli, Stewart's crew chief, is a meticulous workman with exemplary communications skills. The ability of Stewart to convey his orange-and-white Pontiac's handling characteristics to Zipadelli, and Zipadelli's knack for fine tuning based on Stewart's instructions, is a considerable strength. The fact that the two developed their rapport almost instantly, when both were rookies at their respective positions in 1999, is as responsible (Stewart would say more so) for the team's success as the young driver's immense natural talent.

When it came time for the race to be decided, Stewart was right on track, but, by his own admission, enthusiasm betrayed him in the waning laps, and it took a toll on his tires. The track surface at Rockingham is unusually abrasive, in part because of the sandy nature of the area's soil. The sand, whipped up by the wind and all the cars streaking around the track, tends to grind the track surface into a rough, almost pebbly form, and tire wear at Rockingham is typically severe.

Pontiacs took three of the first four positions, quite a reversal from Ford-dominated Daytona, but Stewart had to settle for fourth, behind teammate Labonte, Earnhardt in a Chevrolet, and Ward Burton, who passed Stewart with three laps to go. The four General Motors entries finished as the only cars on the lead lap. Jarrett finished fifth, a lap down, in the highest-placing Ford.

"We worked hard all day at getting the car right, and I just squandered it a little bit at the end by going too hard with the race on the line,"

Stewart said. "I don't know if I could have beaten Bobby (Labonte), but I just got too eager. We probably had a second-place car and finished fourth with it."

The lament was hardly mournful. The entire Joe Gibbs Racing operation had been plagued by ill fortune at Daytona. Labonte's Rockingham victory eased an edge of lingering tension that had been formed at Daytona.

Following the pit-road misadventures that marred the Daytona 500, the tight-knit Gibbs operation had immediately closed ranks, with no public finger-pointing. However, having both cars finish in the top five the following week at Rockingham served the purpose of removing whatever rancor remained from Daytona.

Labonte's torrid pace had enabled him to lead 134 of the 393 laps.

"Well, first of all," said Stewart, "I feel great because my teammate won. Having Bobby for a teammate is like having the Encyclopedia Britannica at your service. If I would have won, I would have felt a little bad just because Bobby didn't, because he had a great car and deserved it, and it would have been a shame if he hadn't won.

"It meant more for this whole operation to get back on track than it did for me to win a race."

Zipadelli was similarly upbeat.

"Our goal for the year is to go to all these tracks and do better than we did on them last year," he said. "We came away from Daytona disappointed at how we did, but the fact remains that we did better than we did the first time we went there in 1999. Then we come here, and we also do better than we did the year before. We finished fourth in the point standings in 1999. If we can keep doing a little better, week after week after week, then we can improve on what we did last season."

4

IT RAINED TOO SOON

LAS VEGAS, Nevada
March 2000

as Vegas can make you, and Las Vegas can break you. Tony Stewart knew the feeling. His career at the racetrack in Vegas resembled a microcosm of the whole Sin City mystique.

Until 1999, Stewart was most noted for his Indy Racing League exploits. He won the pole for the Indianapolis 500, was Rookie of the Year there, and won the IRL points championship in 1997. Las Vegas Motor Speedway was where he clinched that championship, and the year before, it was where Stewart's career nearly came to an end.

A car is said to have "broken loose" when its rear tires lose traction. Stewart suffered multiple injuries when his Indy car broke loose without warning and skittered backward into the retaining wall. Stewart, then 25, was hospitalized for a week and laid-up in his parents' Columbus, Indiana, home for months.

"It was by far the worst thing that ever happened to me in a race car," Stewart recalled. "There was absolutely nothing I could do about it. The car broke loose without any warning and went completely out of control. All I could do was hang on and brace for the impact."

Stewart's first Winston Cup race at the 1.5-mile track had also been a disappointment. He had only three finishes outside the top 25 all year long in 1999, and the first occurred after a "crash" at Las Vegas. ("I didn't crash," Stewart was quick to note. "I got wrecked.")

He was hardly cowed by the rough history, however. "I feel confident because I know my way around this place," he said the day before the CarsDirect.com 400. "I've had my good days here, and I've had my share of bad breaks. I don't really think the past has that much to do with it, though. Honestly, I think the significant thing is that I've had a lot of experience running here, and I feel pretty confident about my ability to do well."

Apart from the bad memories, Stewart felt right at home amidst the Las Vegas glitter. His appearance schedule was tight: he even missed one of the two nights of World of Outlaws sprint-car racing being held at the dirt track behind the "big track's" fourth turn. No, Stewart did not compete—he was still sticking to his vow to give up short tracks—but he thoroughly enjoyed himself hanging out with the dirt trackers.

The CarsDirect.com 400 was NASCAR's third race at Las Vegas Motor Speedway, a 1.5-mile track that had been built by local developers but eventually sold to the Speedway Motorsports Inc. chain headed by Charlotte entrepreneur O. Bruton Smith.

NASCAR team owner Michael Kranefuss noted the importance of Sin City to the stock-car landscape. "Las Vegas is a very unique opportunity," he said. "People who go to Vegas don't necessarily go there because of the races. What little I know of how the community handled things a couple of years ago came from conversations I had with various hotel management people. I think the Las Vegas community did not expect any great rush with last year's race, but, all of a sudden, realized there were about 100,000 people or so coming to their community just because of the races. Obviously, those same people used the same time to see shows and gamble.

"Of the 100,000 people that come here to see the races, and maybe spend a couple of days extra, they are coming from all over the country. It's not just people who live in Las Vegas. I think you're reaching a cross section of population through this race alone. That's important not just to Vegas, but . . . to every sponsor in the series. Because of that, it is vitally important to the race teams, as well."

Stewart's constant companion in Las Vegas was Kara Jobe, the 28-year-old daughter of former Phoenix International Raceway owner Buddy Jobe. Stewart had been playing the field ever since he had called off an engagement with Krista Dwyer the previous fall.

"She [Jobe] understands what this business is like," he marveled later. "When I was out at the World of Outlaws, I was my usual self, hanging out in the pits, kidding around with the guys. I left her by herself a lot of the time, and she was right at home, too. She didn't mind it a bit. I was impressed."

Stewart did manage one costly jaunt through the casino. He did not bring his motor coach to Las Vegas and stayed at the Rio with the team. Rumor had it that he dropped $6,000, mostly at the roulette tables. When chided about the losses, he shrugged. "Hey, it wasn't that long ago that I'd lose $150 and be kicking myself for a week."

Times had changed.

Later, he explained his gambling philosophy. "This is what I've learned," he said. "Before you even go out there, you've got to set a limit on how much you're going to allow yourself to win and how much you're going to lose. If you don't set limits on both ends, you'll end up losing whatever you win."

On race day, the track was brimming with celebrities. Kevin Spacey was on hand. So were Bridget Fonda, the rock group Van Halen, Vince Neil of Motley Crue, and, of course, Wayne Newton.

Picabo Street, the Olympic skier, was planning on cleaning the grille of Stewart's Pontiac Grand Prix during pit stops. Before the race, a Stewart crewman, Jason Shapiro, instructed Street in the niceties of using a pneumatic air gun, and according to Shapiro, she showed bright promise.

The whole atmosphere at the track was markedly different from that of any other stop on the circuit. In the luxury box adjacent to the press box, a blonde wearing little more than a feather boa sat cross-legged, watching the race. Her cheeks had sparkles on them. Newton swept through the garage area, glad-handing everyone in sight, his more-than-jet-black hair looking as if it had been freshly shoe-polished. Lee Greenwood made the national anthem sound as if it had been written by Chuck Berry instead of Francis Scott Key.

Stewart continued his Vegas pattern of good mixed with bad. Saddled with a 16th-place starting spot, he characteristically moved gradually toward the front but ran out of time. Uncharacteristically for the Nevada desert, the race was shortened by rain to 148 of a scheduled 267 laps. Stewart made it into second place, passing Mark Martin, shortly before the rains came. He never led a lap, but Jack Roush, the owner of the Fords that finished first and third, said later he thought Stewart would have won the race had it gone the full distance. Jeff Burton passed Martin on lap 135 and, for the third time in two seasons, won an event shortened by rain.

Perhaps it was modesty, but Stewart disputed the notion that he would have won. "I thought Martin was playing 'possum," said Stewart. "To tell you the truth, when I got past him [Martin], I just thought to myself, he's just biding his time, and he's going to going to come back and beat both of us."

In fact, Martin himself admitted he would not have given up the lead so easily to his teammate Burton, or second to Stewart, had he known heavy rain was imminent.

"I didn't know the weather was going to be like it was," admitted Martin. "I would have tried a little harder to keep the lead if I had known it was about to rain. Nobody told me."

Burton, having won at Las Vegas for the second year in a row, mildly disputed the notion that luck had separated him from his team-mate. "Let's see," he said, "in 1998, they [Martin's team] won seven races and we won two. At that time, I felt like things were working out for him and not for me. Last year, and this year, things have kind of gone my way, but in some ways, that's not true either.

"I've broken more stuff than Mark. I've finished behind him in the points. If you look at both teams and all the finishes, not just the races I've won, you might could look at the whole picture and see that we've had as many bad breaks as they have."

"Maybe Jeff (Burton) pays rent at this track," said Stewart. "Every-body has his niche and the track that he runs good at, and this is one of them for him."

Later, Stewart noted Burton's remarkable knack for winning races shortened by rain. "He's just got it," he quipped. "Whatever he's doing, I'm going to rub up on him, touch him, rub his head or something."

Picabo Street never got to clean Stewart's grille. Because of the rain, he only pitted twice, and the grille never needed cleaning.

While the rain was falling, Stewart lounged comfortably in a luxury box adjacent to the infield media center. Though the likelihood of a second-place finish loomed, without his even getting a shot at racing Burton for the victory, Stewart was relaxed and philosophical.

"Did you see the points?" he said. "If it finishes like this, we're in fourth place. Where were we at this point last year?"

The answer was 25th.

"That's what I mean," he said. "I don't see how you can get upset with that. This is a big week for us."

The overall spectacle, though, was anticlimactic. The race ebbed but never got a chance to flow. When the rains fell, Stewart, who seemed to have the fastest car on the track, had not so much as led a lap. Dale Earnhardt, the fan favorite, had started 33rd and moved his Chevrolet up to eighth by the time of the premature end. Earnhardt said he thought he, too, could have won.

5

SO MANY WALLS, SO LITTLE TIME

HAMPTON, Georgia
March 2000

On a rainy day in the Joe Gibbs Racing transporter, Tony Stewart was in a playful mood. A couple of reporters were on hand for what quickly became a rather irreverent conversation.

"I've got to apologize for having to ask you a question that's rather inane," said the first, thrusting a microcassette recorder in Stewart's direction.

"What's inane mean?" replied Stewart.

"Stupid," the second reporter interjected.

"Oh," said Stewart playfully, "you mean like every other question you ask."

That's Tony. Sometimes he is misunderstood by those who insist on taking life seriously. Mostly, though, he gets along famously with the press, many of whom appreciate a good-humored joust. For those who enjoy unexpected answers, Stewart is the best interview on the NASCAR scene.

"What do you do to concentrate on saving [preserving] tires?"

"Hmm," Stewart said, "I think about what I'm going to have for dinner."

Say what?

"The more you can get your mind off of driving hard, the more you can make yourself relax and try not to abuse the tires any more than you have to, the better off you're going to be. I think about what I want to have for dinner or something silly like that. It gets you in a rhythm. Once you're in a rhythm, you're normally in pretty good shape if you stay there. But as soon as you break that rhythm and have to 'hustle' the car at all, that's when you lose the tenth (of a second) you were going to gain at the end of the run. You lost it by two tenths there.

"You just think of something silly. You might sing a song in your head. Just anything to get yourself in a real calm, smooth rhythm. Once you get yourself in that rhythm, you do everything you can to stay in it."

Oh, OK.

Later, the subject of injured crewman Mike Lingerfelt came up, at which point the conversation turned from the humorous to the almost poignant. Stewart, already four weeks into the season, was still feeling the pain of the pit-road incident in which he had unintentionally and unavoidably run over his front-tire changer. Lingerfelt had been scrambling to retrieve a tire left in Stewart's path by another crew.

"All of our guys have done a pretty good job making adjustments. . . . We brought a new guy in, and he's been working every day at the shop. The new guy's been working real hard to make sure we're up to par . . . but I miss Mikey already. This isn't even the time of the weekend when he's here yet (some crewmen arrive for race day only, since pit stops are not conducted earlier), but I really miss him already. I spent a couple days with him on Monday and Tuesday after he got hurt (in Daytona)."

Stewart assessed some of the challenges of pit stops: "You have two tire carriers who carry two tires in. Why can't they carry two tires out? They talk about us not driving through each other's pit boxes, and it's hard. With the way we have to run the pumps (on a car designed for Daytona or Talladega), the power steering almost goes away when you get down to that low of an RPM. It's hard enough getting into your pit box, let alone getting in, getting squared up, and being able to get out without having to drive through somebody else's box. When you have to drive through somebody else's box, you need help with the tires. Like I say, if two guys can carry two tires in, the same two guys can carry two tires back out with them.

"I think it's a stupid reason to have a guy [Lingerfelt] get injured like that," Stewart added. "He was doing the best he could to keep me from hitting another tire going out of the pits. He threw his body at that tire to get it out of my way. The problem with Mikey is he is so small. He is such a little guy. He's real stout for his size, but he is so little, I never even saw him down there until I hit the tire, and it knocked him up a little bit. He was more worried about me being upset about the whole deal than he was worried about himself. He is a tough guy. He did everything he could do to make sure I got out OK."

By Atlanta, the controversy among Ford, Pontiac, and Chevrolet had reached its usual fever pitch. Drivers of the new Chevrolet Monte Carlo, who'd managed only one top-five finish in the season's first three weeks, had just been allowed to make a modification to the noses of their cars. Some of the cogs in the NASCAR propaganda machine were promoting an old concept, the so called "common templates." With common templates all the body styles would look just alike. (In fact, the term "common templates" was rapidly being supplanted by the even more euphemistic term "aero-matched.")

"From where I sit every Sunday, it all looks the same from the inside," Stewart said. "It doesn't matter to me. I don't really care. As long as it's even for everybody, that's all I care about. NASCAR does a pretty good job of making sure the playing field is level for everyone. It doesn't really concern me either way. Everybody makes such a big deal about it.

"Let NASCAR do its job, and let us go on and worry about racing. You guys [journalists] ask us about body styles and all this and that. I thought all this was about showing up and racing and seeing if you could beat the other 42 guys that you start with on Sunday. I didn't go to college and study aerodynamics or anything, so I don't really know. I just worry about driving the car in all reality."

Then Stewart was asked—again!—about the difficulty he faced in topping the most successful rookie season in NASCAR history.

"I'm not going to try," he retorted. "I'm going to go out and do my job every week, just like I did last year. We'll take the results that it gives us. We didn't have some great master plan last year that got us where we were. We just went and did our work each week.

"It's one of those situations where if it's not broken, don't fix it. We don't think it's broken, so we're not going to try to fix it right now."

The Cracker Barrel 500, won by Chevrolet driver Dale Earnhardt over Stewart's teammate, Bobby Labonte, in a side-by-side finish, was exciting in a derogatory way for Stewart. Race day dawned cool and sunny after a rainy Saturday, but in the abortive qualifying process— the final round was rained out—Stewart fared no better than 27th.

Somehow, Stewart's pit crew managed to cure an early-race engine problem without him losing a lap to the leaders. Subsequent problems caused Stewart to lose two laps in the middle stages, and then the day was ruined by a serious crash. Stewart lost control of his loose car and slid to a halt in a precarious position at the entrance to the 1.54-mile track's trioval (a dogleg in the front stretch). The car sat motionless for a few seconds as approaching drivers tried feverishly to steer clear.

Ford driver Robert Pressley could not avoid Stewart's car and slammed into it at almost full speed. Stewart emerged from the car after a few anxious moments but was obviously shaken as he was helped to the infield hospital.

The 36th-place finish dropped Stewart from fourth to eighth in the point standings. As for the driver's condition, Stewart was unavailable for comment after the race, but his longtime assistant and confidante, Judy Kouba Dominick, made the rounds to say, "Tony's OK. He's just got a devil of a headache."

6

MODEST IMPROVEMENT

DARLINGTON, South Carolina
March 2000

Tony Stewart will win at Darlington Raceway one year. This wasn't it, but the young driver demonstrated the verve necessary to conquer NASCAR's most demanding track.

Darlington is a wonderful anachronism, a track built for the speeds of 1950 by a visionary, not an architect. That man's name was Harold Brasington, and when he came back from the Indianapolis 500 and proclaimed his desire to build a similarly grand facility in what was then a dusty tobacco town, the locals surely must have thought he had taken leave of his senses. Somehow, Brasington built his speedway, and somehow, it still hosts two annual Winston Cup races in a part of the country that is demographically meaningless.

As an Indiana native who grew up with a reverence for "The Speedway"—Indianapolis Motor Speedway—Stewart intuitively understands what Darlington means to the heritage of stock car racing.

"Even though it's just my second year racing down here, I already have a feel for how important Darlington is to the people who have grown up around it," Stewart said. "I didn't grow up around it, but I know that it feels to them the way the Indy 500 feels to me. Being able to be part of that feeling makes it a special place for me to race now."

Like Hoosier Jeff Gordon before him, Stewart did not have an extensive historical perspective of NASCAR when he first came to test his skills on the speedways of the South. He was an "open-wheel guy," but soon he became fascinated with the stock-car culture. "You watch all those old races on Speedvision, and you realize how important races at Darlington have been to this sport," Stewart observed. "To be able to win at Darlington is a great feat, especially with the way the track is abrasive to the tires. It's a hard place to win, so when you can win here, it really means a lot to you."

Like North Carolina Speedway at Rockingham, located little more than an hour's drive away, Darlington's racing surface places harsh demands on racing rubber. The asphalt has a pebbled texture. Driver Sterling Marlin claims he has drawn blood by raking his palm across it. Part of the reason for the coarseness is geographical location. Darlington, about 75 miles inland from the Atlantic Ocean, sits in the middle of a band of sandy soil that stretches across the Carolinas. The soil is mostly sand because, in prehistoric times, the ocean water lapped against what is now called the Sandhills. Today the sand blows across the barren asphalt of Darlington Raceway, carving away at it, and when the 3,400-pound stock cars whip around the track's 1.366-mile circumference, the sand and asphalt act as a grindstone on the custom-built Goodyear rubber.

Stewart observed, "You've got to change your driving style each lap: change where you're lifting, how much you're braking, how much you're on the throttle. It all changes constantly every lap.

"Just depending on what your car is doing, you can run different lines. Some guys, from the beginning of a run (the period over which a set of tires is expended) will race right up against the wall, just because that's where their car feels good. It's not so much, as the run goes on, that you get closer to the wall. It's more dependent on how your car is handling. For instance, my Pontiac might start up there, but there might be another guy who starts his run at the bottom of the track."

Many drivers, for obvious reasons, abhor Darlington. Kyle Petty has occasionally suggested that the track's bowl be flooded and converted into a fishpond. As diligently as racers try to explain Darlington's difficulties in practical terms, competing effectively at the track seems to be more a matter of intuition. Great drivers seem to have a knack for Darlington. There is no more reliable measure of greatness than winning at the track. In its 50-year history, only a few drivers have won at Darlington without winning dozens of races at other places. Some great drivers have never won at Darlington, Rusty Wallace being one modern example. Other legends who never won at the track are Lee Petty and Tim Flock. But even fewer acknowledged non-greats have won there. Larry Frank, in 1962, and Lake Speed, in 1988, pulled off victories that were essentially flukes. Neither ever won again anywhere on the premier circuit, but they each had one glorious after-noon at the track generally accepted as the circuit's most difficult.

The track is shaped like an egg, with the turns on one side, three and four, dramatically narrower than those on the other. The track's racing groove—the part that is usable at speed—is unreasonably narrow.

When Stewart tested at Darlington several weeks in advance of the race, he mainly concentrated on long runs, working on the mysterious challenge of making the tires last longer.

"With the way the track is and how long of a race it is, I really wanted to concentrate on the race setup to see if we could make our car drive well for a long run instead of just the one fast lap that gets you in the race," Stewart said.

All day long during the actual race, Stewart's Pontiac seemed mediocre on new tires. He would fall back, then eventually make his way back into the top five. He never led a lap but never allowed himself to lose sight of the top five, either. With three laps to go, Stewart passed Jeff Burton's Ford to take fourth position, finishing there behind winner Ward Burton (Jeff's older brother) in a Pontiac, Dale Jarrett in a Ford, and Dale Earnhardt in a Chevrolet. When he took the checkered flag, Stewart said to his crew via radio, "If we'd had 25 more laps, guys, we would have won this thing."

The winner was suitably humbled by his first victory in 131 races and second of his career. "Darlington, besides Daytona, is the biggest place to win," Ward Burton said. "This is the place where David Pearson and Richard Petty and Darrell Waltrip and Cale Yarborough and Bobby Allison were winning races when I was growing up.

"To win this race—they say this place is 'too tough to tame'—and we didn't tame it. I just didn't hit anything. This is a tough place to drive, but you've got to have a good car more importantly than anything. To win here is very gratifying."

The top-five finish, his third in five races, elevated Stewart to sixth in the point standings, two positions behind the slot where he completed 1999 but nine positions ahead of his pace at the same point in the previous season. Darlington had been the site of Stewart's first-ever top-10 finish, and he took some post-race satisfaction in reaching a new level of proficiency at the sport's most difficult track.

"We just keep getting better and better here," Stewart said. "That's the main thing. That was our goal. Every time we come back to a track we've been to, we want to be a little better. We finished sixth here last year, and we finished fourth here this year. We're making gains.

"I feel like we're pretty good about everywhere we go," he added, fatigue shortening his sentences. "This was one that needed to be a little better, and that's why we came and tested. I think we're making gains. I'm real happy with the way today went. We kept working hard. The guys did a great job. We kept fighting the racetrack and fighting the sun being in and out. [A car's handling characteristics vary with weather changes]. We changed everything but the steering wheel and the driver. That's what it takes. You've got to be able to keep up, and the guys did a great job of doing that. We've just got to keep working. Every time we come here, we keep getting a little better and a little better, and that was our goal this year. It's just something that only time can take care of. You look at the guys who run good here. They've been here a thousand times. To come here just for our third time, and do what we did today, makes me pretty happy."

Stewart had been in an exuberant mood from the time he arrived three days earlier. He even threatened to participate in the short-track races in nearby Timmonsville the night before the 400-mile race, but it was cold, and Kara Jobe had flown in, and not even Stewart had the audacity to drag her away. When the poor girl had landed at dusk on Saturday, her luggage was nowhere to be found. She and Judy Dominick made a frantic run to the mall in Florence for clothes and makeup.

On race morning, Mike Lingerfelt showed up, his left leg immobilized. He claimed his recovery was ahead of schedule already and told Stewart he would be back to rejoin the pit crew six weeks ahead of the six-month period doctors had recommended for the healing process.

"Tony told me if I insisted on coming back early, he was going to break the other leg," Lingerfelt said, his broken leg propped up on an ice cooler at the Joe Gibbs Racing transporter. "Tony came down to my house [in Marietta, South Carolina] the first day I was home from the hospital," Lingerfelt added, beaming. "I couldn't believe it. Things like that make me want to get back out there."

7

ONE TEMPEST AFTER ANOTHER

BRISTOL, Tennessee
March 2000

Tony Stewart had every reason to be buoyant when he and his team arrived at Bristol Motor Speedway. During the previous season, Bristol had been the first track where Stewart had led a considerable number of laps and the second where he had won a pole, which is the motorsports designation for qualifying first. Of the 21 tracks that host Winston Cup events, Bristol could easily have been considered the next likely site of a Stewart victory. The current season was going well, and by every measure, Stewart was performing better than he had, at the same point, during his rookie season.

Bristol is a track that rewards guts, which Stewart has in abundance. It is also a track where happenstance can sabotage any driver's effort. Someone once said that racing at Bristol, a high-banked, narrow, concrete-surfaced speed bowl, is like "flying jet planes in a gymnasium." No one remembers who originally coined the analogy; at least a dozen drivers have adopted it as their own.

"The fans love this place," said veteran Bill Elliott. "Forty-three cars jammed on a half-mile, high-banked track . . . It's loud, it's definitely full of action, and anything can happen at any given time. From a fan's perspective, it doesn't get much better than Bristol.

"But from a driver's standpoint, it's a whole different ballgame. It's hard on your body, hard on your equipment, hard on your crew, and so much is out of your control. The name of the game is survival, and getting on with it . . . to the next race."

In terms of its atmosphere, Bristol has no equal. "I love the atmosphere of the racetrack," said driver Jimmy Spencer. "I like the way you get treated here, and the fans are just great. They make it exciting. It's not as much a race as it is an event. If I was a fan, and I was paying money to see a race, there's no question that it would be Bristol."

Rusty Wallace, who would defend his title successfully in the Food City 500, is one of only a few drivers who will admit to an affinity for Bristol's coarse concrete, which was first applied to the track in 1992 because track management could not find an asphalt compound that could withstand the pounding of 43 race cars going around the track 500 times twice a year. The problem with concrete is that it lacks the adhesion of asphalt. Bristol features 36-degree banked turns, and the only way to chalk up fast laps is by whipping through those turns at the bottom of the track. A lane up—and there is only about one additional lane—and a driver must slow down to prevent skittering calamitously into the walls.

As a result, NASCAR has no more dazzling spectacle than a Bristol race, which is always fraught with danger. Car owner Bud Moore once said the chief problem with Bristol is "too many damn cars, in too little space, going too damn fast." Twice Bristol races have ended with Dale Earnhardt's Chevrolets colliding with Terry Labonte's Chevies on the very last lap. The first such occasion, in August 1995, saw Labonte take the checkered flag backwards after being hit by Earnhardt as the two exited the final turn. Four years later, Earnhardt again clobbered Labonte from behind, this time with just over a half lap remaining; in that instance, Earnhardt made his way around the track to victory while Labonte's car was being bounced by oncoming traffic on the back stretch. Jeff Gordon's Chevrolet bumped past Wallace's Ford to settle another Bristol contest in April 1997.

In 1999, his rookie year on the Winston Cup circuit, Stewart led 54 laps at Bristol, only to be eliminated from contention when the lapped car driven by Jerry Nadeau spun out in front of the lead pack. Wallace missed the melee, but four others, most notably Stewart and Jeff Gordon, did not. That was the weekend when writers and fans began telling one another about the rookie driver who was obviously capable of competing on an even basis with the NASCAR who's who.

"I love this place," said Stewart, who was among the fastest in Friday's practice sessions. "It reminds me of Winchester and Salem, the high-banked tracks I raced on back in the Midwest. Maybe that's why I like coming here. It takes a real gut check to race on tracks like this, where anything can happen at any time."

Shortly, some of those things started happening. The qualifying performance was disappointing. Stewart had only the 19th fastest time, and he blamed himself. In the lounge area, at the front of the transporter, Stewart threw a tantrum that involved harsh words and the hurling of inanimate objects. Crewmen rolled their eyes and exchanged knowing smiles; they shrugged and said things like, "You know Tony . . . he hates to lose." Greg Zipadelli, the crew chief, patiently went about his business, letting Stewart expunge his demons.

Saturday was no better. Barely a lap into the morning practice, Stewart's engine blew, leaving a trail of oil in its wake. Stewart wrestled the car to a complete stop only inches away from the retaining wall. The engine would still have to be replaced, but he'd managed to save the rest of the car. In doing so, he had avoided having to roll out the backup car, which would have meant dropping to the rear of the 43-car field for the start of Sunday's race.

"The only reason I parked it up there," said Stewart, "was so that I wouldn't drop oil all over for all the other guys to get into. I just figured it was better to sit tight and make sure everybody behind me got through okay."

On Sunday, mechanical bugaboos struck again. As Stewart expected, he was able to move up quickly at the start. He had carved what appeared to be a solid presence in the top five when, once again, on lap 72, the engine failed. When Stewart coasted to a halt in the pit lane, the crew swarmed the orange-and-white Pontiac. Soon Jason Shapiro discovered the culprit. A belt had broken, probably from being hit by a piece of debris thrown up from the concrete as Stewart whizzed by. At speed, the sudden loss had caused the engine, almost immediately, to overheat. After several minutes of tense work, a new belt was secured in place. The engine problem was, however, terminal. Stewart completed only one more lap. In the final finishing order, Stewart's name was 42nd in a field of 43, the worst finish of his career. Afterward, a still-steaming Stewart had almost nothing to say.

"I know sometimes it gets me in trouble when I get frustrated," he said later, "but I almost think it's a necessary part of being a competitor. If I didn't have this passion, if I didn't want to win so badly, I can't help but think I wouldn't do as well as I do.

"I think I'm supposed to get angry when things are rotten. I don't like being angry, but I wouldn't like myself if I could accept losing, either."

Wallace won the Food City 500 for the second straight year, marking the 50th victory of the 43-year-old driver's career. He had been waiting for almost a year.

"It got to be almost where it was a jinx," Wallace said. "We kept talking about number fifty, and the wins just wouldn't come. Some weird things would happen."

8

RUMORS START TO FLY

JUSTIN, Texas
April 2000

In the short history (1997-present) of NASCAR racing at Texas Motor Speedway, disorder has been the rule rather than the exception. The 1.5-mile track, built to resemble other Speedway Motorsports, Inc., tracks near Charlotte and Atlanta, has been plagued by problems: the parking lots flooded in 1997, and water seeped up through cracks in the pavement in '98.

The mood at Joe Gibbs Racing rather reflected the track's history, at least where Tony Stewart's Home Depot operation was concerned. Stewart was coming off the worst performance of his career, a 42nd place at Bristol that had dropped him from sixth to 12th in the all-important point standings.

Farfetched rumors suggested that Gibbs was thinking about switching from Pontiacs to Fords. The rumors heated up when Stewart performed poorly in qualifying. When the final round of time trials was rained out, Stewart had to take a provisional starting spot, meaning that he began the race 38th in a field of 43. The provisional system is one in which NASCAR awards the final seven spots in the starting field to teams based on their positions in the car-owner point standings.

In general, it rewards teams that participate in the entire 34-race schedule.

Having no control over management decisions concerning the brand of car or equipment used by the Gibbs team, Stewart adopted his usual position of staying above the fray. "Hey, guys, I just drive the cars," he said. "It's not my responsibility to decide which car we run, or even how the car is prepared. I'm not the expert there. Joe Gibbs and Greg Zipadelli are a lot better qualified to make decisions like that, and I've got enough confidence in them to trust their judgment. I'll take whatever they decide to put me in and do the best I can with it."

Apparently the team's purchase of several Taurus bodies had spurred the Ford rumors. However, a switch was not being pondered. The team was simply responding to the possibility that NASCAR might be moving toward so-called common templates. Frustrated at the week-to-week difficulty in making rules that ensured each of the three makes—Ford, Chevrolet, and Pontiac—was relatively equal in terms of aerodynamics, NASCAR had been exploring the possibility of requiring similarly shaped cars. It was a controversial plan, particularly among the three manufacturers, but it had become the overriding technical issue of the season. Jimmy Makar, overall manager of the Gibbs stock car racing operation and Bobby Labonte's crew chief, had merely been hedging the team's bets. According to rumors, the common templates were going to be at least loosely based on the configuration of the Taurus.

"I just don't care," said Stewart, "and I think it's in my best interest not to care. I'm committed to Joe Gibbs Racing, and whatever the team decides to do is fine with me."

Such responses were not overly popular and only grudgingly accepted by many reporters covering the weekend's events. "I can't help that," said Stewart. "My policy is just to say what I think. There's nothing there to read into it. I don't have any hidden agendas. I'm just a racer."

Unlike some fellow drivers, Stewart felt comfortable with the actual track. "I've run here in a Busch car, an IRL (Indy Racing League) car, and in a Cup car," he said. "I never looked at it as a treacherous racetrack. It's so fast, and with the fresh pavement, it has a lot of grip in it. For some reason, it seems that the track's transitions are very line-sensitive."

By "line-sensitive," Stewart meant the course, or line, taken by each driver around the track. Different drivers take different lines based on their individual styles.

"The corners' exits and entries are very tricky," he added, "and that's what makes Texas difficult. I don't think it's treacherous. You just have to hit your marks every lap. Texas doesn't leave a whole lot of room for error."

Stewart has consistently held that his broad-based experience is less of an advantage than most observers figure. At Texas, as at other tracks like Indianapolis, Loudon (New Hampshire), and Phoenix, he did not consider it a particular advantage to have driven at a track in both open-wheel and stock cars.

"The IRL was nothing like driving a stock car," he said. "You could go anywhere on the track that you wanted to with the IRL car. It was as easy as riding down the interstate, whereas, with the Cup car, you're not off the gas very long, but you do have to 'lift.' With the track being so line-sensitive, it's really important that you're doing the same thing every lap and making sure you're very consistent in how you're driving the car."

As usual, with his race setup on the car—teams set up their chassis

quite differently for the one- or two-lap bursts required in qualifying—
Stewart moved quickly through the field. Unfortunately, on his second
pit stop, a NASCAR-assessed penalty cost him a lap. Stewart was
pitting at the head of pit row, near turn four, when one of his used
tires squirted away and rolled across pit road into the grassy area that
separated the pits from the track's "tri-oval." As punishment for the
miscue, a NASCAR official stood in front of the car, holding Stewart
for 15 seconds before allowing him to return to the track.

Stewart recovered nicely and drove his way past the leaders to get
back on the lead lap in time for the race's latter stages. After reaching
sixth place with about 20 laps to go, Stewart had some late handling
problems that relegated him to a ninth-place finish, still not bad considering that he had started 38th.

Dale Earnhardt Jr., two-time Busch Series champion and son of
the late seven-time Winston Cup champ, became the second rookie
in as many years to win a Cup race. Stewart's three 1999 victories had
marked the first time a rookie had won in NASCAR's top series
since 1987.

Earnhardt Jr. won his first race 21 years and one day after his
father's first victory, on April 1, 1979, in Bristol. The third-generation
driver also won his first Cup race at the site of his first victory in the
Busch Grand National Division, on April 4, 1998. Earnhardt Jr. won
his 16th race in the Busch Series and his 12th in Winston Cup. The
Earnhardts became the fifth set of father-and-son winners in the history
of NASCAR's premier division, joining the Allisons (Bobby and Davey), the Bakers (Buck and Buddy), the Jarretts (Ned and Dale), and
the Pettys (Richard and Kyle).

Even before the season started, Stewart had predicted that the
rookie class, which included long-time Indy-car driver Scott Pruett,
Earnhardt Jr., and Matt Kenseth, would fare well.

"I thought it would have been before this," Stewart said. "I think he is right on schedule right now, and I don't think that is the only one he'll get this year."

Stewart's remark would prove prophetic in a rather painful way.

Earnhardt Jr. said, "I think at least a couple of rookies will get into victory lane this year."

He, too, would be right.

9

A PLACE HE LOVES TO HATE

MARTINSVILLE, Virginia
April 2000

O n April 18, 1999, Tony Stewart's first visit to Martinsville Speed-way, he won the first pole of his career. Stewart had completed a lap at an average speed of 95.275 miles per hour, a track record.

Before that race, Stewart gave no indication of a milestone perfor-mance. After his first test session, Stewart had expressed puzzlement with the narrow, almost paper-clip-shaped track, NASCAR's shortest.

"I don't think I've ever been in a test before where I learned almost nothing," he had said. "I went up there and spent a day turning laps around that place, and now that it's over, I can honestly say that I don't have a clue."

Then he set the track record.

On the Saturday night before the Sunday race, Stewart had attended a local short-track race at 311 Speedway in Madison, North Carolina, just across the state line from the southern Virginia track. He had arrived in nondescript street clothes. It's unusual to see a race driver in clothing that does not feature some reference to one or more of his sponsors, but Stewart had come to watch others race, not make a promotional appearance. When a driver from one of the lower divi-sions—dirt tracks routinely feature three or more different classes—

49

showed up in the grandstands wearing his uniform, fans quickly gathered for conversation and even an autograph or two. Meanwhile, maybe five rows away sat one of the more famous motorsports figures in America, and no one even noticed. By 2000, such anonymity would be much more difficult for Stewart to pull off.

On that cold night in 1999, Stewart had been asked how he felt about the race, the Goody's Body Pain 500, which would transpire the following day. "I'd say we're probably going to drop like a rock," he said, explaining that "happy hour," the final Winston Cup practice session, had gone poorly. "Qualifying is one thing, but with a race setup, out there on the track with all the other cars, I don't know what I'm doing."

The remark seemed overly modest considering his stellar qualifying performance. "You realize, Tony," the journalist said, "that if you go out there and win that race tomorrow, I'm never going to believe another word that you say, as long as you live."

"I'd say you don't have a thing to worry about," Stewart said, laughing. "If I win that race tomorrow, I won't trust myself anymore."

The next day, in his first race at Martinsville, Stewart restored his credibility while perhaps diminishing his reputation. He finished 20th, two laps behind winner John Andretti.

The second Martinsville event, the NAPA Autocare 500 on October 3, 1999, turned out to be Stewart's worst performance of his rookie season. It was also the occasion of perhaps his most famous moment. Early in the race, Stewart had been attempting to move up from a 37th starting position, one of only two times all year he had been forced to accept a provisional starting spot. While closing in on the top 25, Stewart felt that a longtime rival, Kenny Irwin, was blocking him. After several laps of tight competition, Stewart's Pontiac bumped Irwin's Ford, which spun out. Happenstance later brought the two back together, and Stewart tapped Irwin again, and Irwin again spun out. Stewart claimed later that both incidents were inadvertent.

A third confrontation between the two seemed quite intentional, the principal difference being that Stewart, not Irwin, was in front. Angered at the two prior incidents, Irwin rammed Stewart's car and didn't back off when the orange Pontiac skidded out of control. Stewart's car was virtually destroyed, and when he climbed out of the smoking car and removed his helmet, his eyes were black as coal. With every person in the crowded grandstands watching, Stewart waited for Irwin's car, damaged only mildly, to come back around. Stewart, a lefty, removed the glove-like heat pads from his shoes and fired them at Irwin's windshield. Irwin stopped for some almost-surely profane remark of the "that's what you get" variety. Stewart then leaned into the passenger-side window of Irwin's black Ford and tried to get at Irwin, who accelerated and spun Stewart back out onto the track. A healthy percentage of the nation's newspapers featured photographs of the incident the following morning.

The 1999 pole notwithstanding, Martinsville's .526-mile track is Stewart's least favorite. "It's like racing around a parking lot with a curb around it," he said the morning of Pole Day for the 2000 Goody's Body Pain 500.

"I haven't loved it yet. I still hate it. If it's a love-hate relationship, then we're missing the 'love' part of the equation. The people here make it fun because they're really enthusiastic. That makes racing here fun, but the track is just a tricky place to get around."

The previous autumn, the Martinsville crowd, particularly those ringing the first and second turns, had roared their approval of Stewart's impulsive actions during the Irwin incident. The incident had, in fact, made him a fan favorite at the track.

Despite his misgivings about the track itself, Stewart was in a fine mood on Friday before qualifying. He was even willing to discuss his previously guarded belief that, despite some early-season success, Pontiacs were operating at a disadvantage compared to the newer models debuted by Chevrolet and Ford at Daytona. NASCAR had responded to early-season complaints from the Chevy forces by extending the nose of the new Monte Carlo's racing configuration by two inches. That seemingly small adjustment had brought almost immediate results, including victories by both Dale Earnhardt and Dale Earnhardt Jr. in a span of four races. Meanwhile, the Pontiacs had been left with the same aerodynamic specifications with which they had closed the previous season.

One week after he had vowed to leave the politicking to others, Stewart abruptly broke his silence. "They say they are going by the wind-tunnel tests," groused Stewart, referring to NASCAR, "and yet, those tests (conducted just prior to the Atlanta race that Earnhardt had won) show that the Fords and Chevys are close, but we're about 20 percent off. You go to them, and they say, 'Well, look at the results.' Wait a minute. A minute ago you said you were going by the wind-tunnel tests. Why should we be penalized just because we've won a few races (two, one each by Bobby Labonte and Ward Burton)? If NASCAR says it wants a level playing field, and that's the term they always use, shouldn't they give the teams cars that are equal and then let them make the best of it? What are we supposed to do? Lose on purpose?"

Later that afternoon, Stewart's qualifying performance was awful, and he wound up taking a provisional slot in the starting lineup for the second week in a row. His sunny disposition quickly evaporated. When Motor Racing Network (MRN) reporter Joe Moore walked up to Stewart and, on live radio, asked him why he had done so much worse than the previous year, Stewart turned and strode into the Joe Gibbs Racing transporter without a word.

The next morning he defended his action. "He (Moore) never gave me any warning," Stewart said. "He just stuck a mike in front of my face. Those guys from MRN can be awfully inconsiderate. When [rival network] PRN [Performance Racing Network, operated by Bruton Smith's Speedway Motorsports] broadcasts the races, their guys always visit with you and give you a chance to get to know them. At the very least, they let you know they're about to put you on the air. I wasn't prepared, and basically he just asked a question that meant, 'Why do you suck?' It made me mad, but I'm sure it's going to get me in trouble."

Moore, by the way, took Stewart's action and subsequent remarks constructively. They later settled their differences amicably, with Moore telling Stewart he would try not to put Stewart on the spot—no more unannounced live radio interviews.

Stewart had some frank remarks for reporters that day. "It's not very politically correct to talk about it, but I know exactly what's wrong with our qualifying performance. It's no secret that the problem is the four things that connect the car to the racetrack."

His obvious reference to his tires enraged the officials of Goodyear Tire and Rubber Company, the exclusive suppliers of racing tires to Winston Cup and most other NASCAR series. Freedom of speech is not Goodyear's favorite part of the Constitution. Rumor has it that the tire company has punished its critics by furnishing certain teams with its culls, tires that are not up to par. What Goodyear unquestionably does is encourage the use of politically correct terms and definitions in reference to its products. For instance, rarely does a driver refer to "blowing" a tire. The correct term, to Goodyear's way of thinking, is "cutting" a tire, the implication being that the tire's failure resulted from a defect unrelated to its manufacture. Any driver who says he "blew" a tire can expect a visit from a representative of the company.

Oddly enough, Stewart wasn't actually complaining about the tire's reliability or even its quality. The tire design brought to Martinsville by Goodyear—only a single, uniform model is allowed in any given race—was different from the previous year's design. From Stewart's vantage point, the different design made the previous year's performance data useless. The team's notes on chassis setup were obsolete, and in an age in which the difference between the fastest and slowest qualifiers is typically a half-second or less in lap time, Stewart's team had been unable to adjust adequately during pre-qualifying practice sessions.

Still, the self-described "World Leader in Tires" did not take Stewart's remarks nearly as constructively as had radio announcer Joe Moore. Stewart's team had been one of a select number getting its tires free from Goodyear. That courtesy ended a week after the Martinsville race. The cost of Stewart's outspokenness, in terms of Joe Gibbs Racing's budget, was an estimated $250,000 for the season.

"I never said they didn't have a good tire," said Stewart. "I just said the tires were the big reason I didn't qualify better."

On race day, Stewart briefly put to rest the controversy. From the moment the field took the green flag, Stewart's performance was splendid. He drove up through the field impressively, evincing not a hint of the impatience of the previous autumn. Stewart finished sixth in a race won, surprisingly, by Mark Martin, another driver who admittedly dislikes the track, in a Ford.

"We kept working on the car and kept trying things, found a couple things we liked, and just stuck with it all day," said Stewart. "This is what we needed, by far our best run here. If I can run like that here, I think we're going to have a pretty good rest-of-the-season now."

Martin, by his own admission, stole the race from Rusty Wallace, who led 334 of the 500 laps only to botch things with a poor strategic decision. On the 437th lap, Wallace elected to pit for four tires during a yellow-flag period. Four drivers—Martin, Jeff Burton, John Andretti, and Michael Waltrip—didn't pit. Four others—Dale Jarrett, Jeff Gordon, Bobby Hamilton, and Jeremy Mayfield—pitted for two tires and beat Wallace out of the pits. As a result, the race's dominant driver fell all the way to 10th place, and finished there, thanks in part to a bumping incident with Hamilton that occurred with 12 laps remaining.

"I don't know how I beat Jeff [Burton, the runner-up]. I know he's a better driver than me at Martinsville Speedway," said Martin. "Rusty is a lot better driver than me. I'm so terrible at Martinsville that it says a lot about this team that they could win with me driving it."

Martinsville, the oldest track on the schedule, traditionally presents each race winner with a grandfather clock. "My wife has nagged me about one of these grandfather clocks for about 10 years," Martin said.

Wallace lamented letting the race slip away. "It was just real upsetting to have that dominant a car. . . . I really thought, with 70 (actually 63) laps to go, we needed to get [four] tires on. I didn't think a bunch of them would just stay out like they did, but they did. I got behind, my car pushed [turned poorly], and I just couldn't get back around them."

10

TROUBLE FROM ALL SIDES

TALLADEGA, Alabama
April 2000

sn't Tony Stewart just what a racer is supposed to be?

Once upon a time, yes, but as the Winston Cup teams arrived at another fabled old venue—Talladega Superspeedway in the rolling hills of eastern Alabama—the breath of fresh air seemed in many quarters to have turned into a bitter wind. Stewart was under fire from all sides, and many of his detractors had once praised him for the very virtues they now disparaged.

Though neither the officials of Goodyear nor Joe Gibbs Racing much wanted to talk about it, word of Stewart's revoked free-tire deal was making the rounds of the Talladega Superspeedway garage area. Some members of Stewart's own team expressed their misgivings and frustrations with the consequences of the driver's outspokenness.

Stewart also made some indelicate remarks toward Chevrolet, opining that he thought NASCAR largesse had turned the Monte Carlo into the superior make. "The Chevrolets ought to be stout at Talladega because they're essentially running a Late Model body [Late Model is a short-track class, i.e., a body with fewer similarities to its passenger-car equivalent] with the nose being stuck out as far as it is," he said.

"We're just kind of stuck with what we've got [a Pontiac]. We need to do the best we can with what we have."

It would have been more tactful for Stewart to have criticized the Ford Taurus—Chevrolet and Pontiac both being General Motors products—but Stewart, as usual, said what he thought.

Eight races into the season, Stewart was a disappointing 10th in the series' point standings. He had not won a race. In fact, he had not led a lap. He had finished in the top 10 five times, but the remarkable consistency of the previous year had disappeared. Was he having a bad season? Only by the expectations generated in his rookie year.

Stewart needed a respite from the suffocating effect of the season. Talladega was an unlikely oasis. "I never liked restrictor-plate racing anyway," said Stewart with his trademark frankness. "I don't think it's real racing to begin with."

The restrictor-plate mess began at Talladega, at least in its modern incarnation. The horsepower-sapping plates, applied between carburetor and intake manifold [yes, NASCAR engines still use the carburetors that are now obsolete in passenger cars], were mandated for the 1988 season because of a horrifying crash in July 1987. In the Talladega 500, a Buick driven by Bobby Allison, one of the sport's all-time greats, bounced crazily into the air after being tapped from behind by another car. At the incredible speeds then being run at the gigantic track—Bill Elliott had averaged 203.827 mph to win the pole for that particular race—Allison's gold car shot into the air, briefly began spinning almost like a top on its nose, then slammed into the reinforced fencing separating the track from the grandstands. Allison's car ripped out about 150 feet of the fence, but almost miraculously, the spinning car did not bounce into the crowded grandstand.

The following February, when the 1988 season began, restrictor plates became mandatory at 2.5-mile, high-banked Daytona and at 2.66-mile, even-higher-banked Talladega.

While the plates may have made the races safer for fans, they have made them more dangerous for drivers by robbing them of throttle response. Before restrictor plates, engine power enabled cars to slingshot past one another in the draft. One car would tuck itself in behind the other, taking advantage of the draft, or slipstream, of the leading car. A deft move out of the draft would cause an interruption in the wind pocket, and the power of the engine would enable the second car to shoot past the defenseless first car. The breathtaking maneuver was used dozens of times in each race by cars running in every portion of the field.

Since 1988, the famed "slingshot" maneuver has all but disappeared because the engines, reduced from 700-800 horsepower to 380-450, no longer have the power to pull it off. Now the lead car has the advantage, and the only practical means of passing is by cooperation from others. Two or three cars "drafting" together can move in unison—drivers signal to each other via hand signals, and sometimes agreements are forged on pit road and radioed to drivers—to pass one car speeding alone. Two factors—power and aerodynamics—cause race cars to go fast, and restrictor plates have made aerodynamics by far the more important factor at Daytona and Talladega.

Another result of restrictor plates is the increasingly tight proximity of cars. Once a race at Talladega consisted of individual packs of cars, perhaps 10-12 in a bunch, running at various places on the track. With the advent of restrictor plates, cars lost the horsepower necessary to "escape" one another. By the mid-1990s, it was no longer unusual to see the entire 43-car field running inches apart for lap after lap, sometimes in two, three, even four parallel rows. If a driver makes the slightest mistake, such as a failed attempt to move from one row to the next, the resulting crashes frequently collect as many as 20 cars in frightful displays. Though no drivers have been killed at Talladega in recent years, injuries abound. Two of the sport's bigger names, Dale Earnhardt, before his fatal 2001 crash, and Bill Elliott, had experienced career slumps due in no small part to serious injuries suffered in Talladega races.

"Talladega is the most nerve-wracking experience that you can go through as a driver, especially if you're about 15th in the pack with around five laps to go," Stewart said. "There are so many things going on around you that . . . [in 1999] I was four-wide, and I was on the outside of the four-wide pack. So, there was me, and the concrete wall, and the concrete was about a foot away from me, and the guy on the inside of me was about three or four inches away. I can only imagine what the middle two guys felt like. You've got cars behind you, you've got cars in front of you, and you're running 195 miles an hour. It's just nerve-wracking."

Still, having finished fifth and sixth in his only previous starts at Talladega, Stewart seemed to be in an excellent position to build momentum. "It's a pretty humbling experience," he said, discounting his previous finishes. "Every practice session you go out there and realize how little you know about it and how much more there really is to know, but the hard thing is that you can't go to a test session to learn that. You can't get 40 cars to go to a test with you so you can learn what you need to learn. It's trial and error in the practice sessions and in the race. You just try to pick up as much as you can. The important thing for me is that I try to learn something at each restrictor-plate race so that I'm better for the next one.

"There have been so many times when I've thought that I had a big enough run on a guy, and I thought some guys would go with me, that I pulled out, but I quickly found out I would have been better off staying in line. I stay in line a lot more now than I used to. Every time someone pulls out, he gets shuffled to the back, and I end up gaining a spot. It's a process that's tough to figure out. There are only about four guys who have figured it out and really know how to do it right: Dale Earnhardt, Jeff Gordon, Dale Jarrett, and Bobby Labonte."

Patience, Stewart said, "is the gospel, basically. There are a lot of times when you think you can pull out and pass, but if you do, once you get there, you realize that you can't pass. It makes it real critical that you take your time and that you don't get caught up in trying to make a move too fast. Just stay in line, and sometimes you'll have more patience than 20 other guys."

The trouble, both for Stewart and teammate Bobby Labonte, was that they began the DieHard 500 buried deep in the field. In a remarkable coincidence, the engines of both drivers developed "misses" during their qualifying runs. Examinations uncovered the same flaws deep beneath the cylinder heads. As a result, Labonte, still leading the point standings, began the race in 37th position, with Stewart starting 39th. Stewart thus used his third provisional in as many weeks. He had needed only two during the entire 1999 season.

For Stewart, restrictor-plate racing became dull as he and his teammate attempted to make their way up through the field. "It was so boring," Stewart said. "I told Bobby that, since I started behind him at the beginning of the race, that wherever he went, I went. That's what our game plan was at the start. We went through the first two thirds of the race that way. Everywhere he went on the track, I'd follow him."

In the first 120 of the 188 laps, Stewart and Labonte spent most of the time outside the top 20, but their plan was to put themselves in position to make a run at the front in the final 50 laps, there being no great benefit to taking chances in the draft before the late stages. The plan seemed to be working. Both were running between the 10th and 16th positions in the laps leading up the race's most significant moment.

"At one point, we were kind of at the back of the pack and had a little gap back there, just to make sure that if something happened, we had plenty of time to react," Stewart recalled later. "I just kind of got bored and pulled up beside Bobby and waved to him, then dropped back in line. He was so comfortable in his car that he switched over to our [radio] frequency and started talking to me.

"He just kind of explained that there were some guys up ahead doing some things that might get ugly in a couple of laps, so we were just back there being patient. Sure enough, when it came time to race at the end, the big wreck happened."

At lap 138, in the curved section of the track known as the trioval, former open-wheel stars Robby Gordon and Scott Pruett, both driving Fords, collided with each other. It was Pruett who lost control: he said later that he was tapped from behind by another Taurus, driven by Jeremy Mayfield. For whatever reason, Pruett's car skidded to the left into Gordon's, which in turn clobbered the Chevrolet of Michael Waltrip, and from there the chain reaction engulfed 16 cars, including both Labonte's and Stewart's. Labonte, trying to make his way through the smoke, slammed into the already damaged Pontiac of his teammate. Stewart's car burst into flames as it came to an agonizing halt, but he had not been shaken up and easily clambered out.

"Bobby and I rode around at three-quarter throttle most of the day just waiting ... waiting for a wreck to happen," Stewart said. "You make your last pit stop and you go back out, and then you get caught in it when it's time to go racing. We tried to be careful all day, and as soon as it was time to go, then we got in that wreck. It's just frustrating. I wouldn't call that real racing. It's not real racing, but it's real entertaining, I guess."

The crash consigned Stewart to a 34th-place finish and cost Labonte the points lead. Stewart dropped from 10th to 13th, his lowest ranking in the season standings since March 1999.

"The wreck started so far in front of me that I couldn't see anything," Stewart said. "All I could do was just go off my spotter [a team member stationed at a vantage point where he can advise the driver via two-way radio]. He had the best viewpoint. He just kept saying, 'Stay high, stay high.' I was as far up as I could go. I don't even know if I got hit from behind, if that's what turned the car around, or whether getting into cars in front of me turned it. It's just typical restrictor-plate racing."

Jeff Gordon broke a losing streak of his own at Talladega, winning the DieHard 500 after 13 fruitless weeks that began in October 1999. Gordon, in fact, had posted only his first top-five finish of the 2000 season the week before in Martinsville.

Gordon became the ninth different winner in as many races. He also succeeded where Stewart and Labonte had failed, driving to victory after starting 36th—only one position ahead of Labonte and three ahead of Stewart.

The frenetic nature of that accomplishment was not lost on Gordon. "I was stacked up there a couple of times, just shaking my head in disbelief," Gordon said. "I know it's awesome for the fans to see that, and when it's all over and everybody comes out of it safe, we all kind of shake our heads, but I can tell you, while I'm doing it, it's not a very fun feeling."

"The restrictor plates have got everybody slowed down and jammed up," added Dale Earnhardt. "It's getting worse and worse. The more they slow horsepower down, the more we run side-by-side, and 'beat and bam' trying to get where we've got to go."

One newspaper report termed it "high-speed Tetris."

"It's worse than it's ever been, as far as there being no way to pull out [to pass]," Earnhardt added. "Everybody has got to find somebody to help him. It was just a tough, tough day. You can't pull out and go, and that creates a lot of problems. If that's what [NASCAR] wants, then that's what they've got.

"It was just a terrible, terrible mental deal to try to run in the drafts with anybody. You could not stay out front. People were 'chunking' you in the rear to get by you. . . . This is superspeedway racing, but it sure was a bunch of 'bumper cars.' It was as bad as Martinsville as far as getting the contact we had. I about got spun out two or three times down the straightaway. . . . It's gone from speedway racing to Martinsville short-track racing here at Talladega."

Kyle Petty, who had his best finish of the year (ninth), said, "Any time you miss a wreck at Talladega, it's not your driving ability. It's God looking after you, man, I'm telling you."

At the end of the Talladega debacle, Stewart clearly needed a break. Naturally, he took it at a racetrack.

Stewart's obsession with his sport is practically all-encompassing. While he enjoys fishing, he admitted that, in the eight months since he had purchased an expensive bass boat—the model in question has more power than many passenger cars—he had taken it out on Lake Norman exactly twice. Stewart also enjoys bowling, supposedly, but he could not recall his average. His interest in golf consists mainly of playing it enough to be qualified to ridicule it. Other than a handful of charity tournaments, Stewart has visited the links only once, when he and a crony amused themselves one night after a midget-car feature by attempting to play several holes in the darkness.

Yes, Stewart does maintain an avid interest in women, but it is instructive to note that the cancellation of his engagement to Krista Dwyer the previous autumn had more than a little to do with her intrusions on his time at the track "with the guys." Ideally, Stewart would race every day, but unlike many other drivers, he is also a fan. Visitors to his team's transporter or his motorcoach often find Stewart watching a Formula One race, or CART qualifying, via satellite television. He has shown up unannounced at every manner of track, even to watch kids in go-karts or quarter-midgets. In fact, Stewart would much prefer going to a short track and paying his way in rather than being paid to show up and sign autographs.

So . . . Stewart spent Easter weekend at the Indy Racing Northern Lights Series event in Las Vegas. He co-owns a regular entry in the series, previously known as the Indy Racing League, in which he won a championship in 1997. Stewart, Larry Curry (the crew chief during his IRL days), Curry's wife Bobbi, Rick Ehrgott, and Andy Card are partners in Tri Star Motorsports. Dr. Jack Miller, like Stewart a Hoosier but unlike Stewart a dentist, was driver of the team's Dallara-Oldsmobile.

For the second time in 2000, Stewart handled crew-chief duties for his Indy car. He had also provided similar instruction at the series' season opener in January at Walt Disney World Speedway in Lake Buena Vista, Florida, when Robby Unser had been the team's driver. "Dr. Jack" fell out of the race after only 54 of a scheduled 208 laps in the Vegas Indy 300, placing 24th in a field of 28.

"It's just a different set of challenges," Stewart said, "and it's a lot of fun. I've been racing 21 years, and now I'm at a point in my career where I'm able to do some different things. To be a car owner with Larry, Rick, and Andy, that part, by itself, is a lot of fun for me. I can't be there a lot.

"Coming [to Las Vegas] and being a crew chief adds a little more stress to the weekend, but I know, after I did it at Orlando [near the Disney track], and I'm sure after I do it this time, I'll have a greater appreciation for what my crew chief does for me on the Cup Series."

Stewart said that while he would not duplicate his much ballyhooed feat of running the Indianapolis 500 and Coca-Cola 600 on the same day, as he had in 1999, he did plan on attending the 500 and probably playing crew chief again in the world's most famous race.

After all, what would Memorial Day weekend be without a frantic plane flight to Charlotte for the 6 p.m. start of the 600?

11

FRUSTRATIONS MOUNT

FONTANA, Calif.
April 2000

alifornia Speedway represented a pleasant diversion for Tony Stewart. Though he was born and raised in Indiana, the Golden State's long tradition of open-wheel competition had brought Stewart to its rural dirt tracks many times while he was driving sprint cars and midgets. The West Coast had produced innumerable Indy-car stars—Bill Vukovich, Troy Ruttman, and Parnelli Jones among them—and Stewart had many friends there.

"I normally see a lot of those guys during both of our trips to California," Stewart said [the Winston Cup Series also makes an annual visit to the Sears Point road course north of San Francisco]. "That's part of the fun in going out to California and the West Coast: being able to see a lot of the guys that I raced sprint cars and midgets with. It always feels good to come back out here just from that standpoint."

Following the path blazed first by Jeff Gordon and later by Stewart, more and more open-wheel stars are beginning to consider stock car racing as their major league. Former World of Outlaws sprint-car champion Dave Blaney had completed a Busch Grand National apprenticeship and was struggling to make the adjustment to being a Winston Cup rookie. A Stewart protégé, fellow Hoosier Jason Leffler, had moved into the second-rung BGN circuit in a Pontiac owned by Stewart's owner, Joe Gibbs.

"I think it's because NASCAR owners don't care how much money you have," said Stewart. "They go out and get the sponsorships, and then they look for the best drivers, where, in Indy-car racing, if a driver could come up with a million dollars or two million dollars, then he could go run Indy.

"Guys like myself and Dave Blaney and Jeff Gordon, we didn't have a couple million dollars in our back pockets to go run Indy. We weren't in the business world, so we didn't know how to even approach somebody to get that kind of money. It was like standing behind a 40-foot, chain-link, electrical fence. There was no way you were going to get through it. There were a lot of car owners down here [in NASCAR] who looked at us as just drivers, and not people who carried big wallets."

Stewart also shed some light on why he had adapted so quickly to the high level of competition in the Winston Cup Series. He had never won a Busch race in more than a full season of trying, yet he had immediately won three times as a Cup rookie and finished fourth in the series standings.

"I was used to driving cars with higher horsepower," Stewart said. "The midgets didn't have a ton of horsepower, but the horsepower-to-weight ratio was around three to one. With a sprint car, you've got about 800 horsepower, and they only weigh around 1,100 pounds. Learning to deal with all that horsepower in the Winston Cup car was something that was already familiar to me."

Stewart made an abrupt decision, hastily rearranging his schedule. On the Saturday night before the NAPA Auto Parts 500, he would race at Irwindale Speedway, a half-mile paved oval located only about a half-hour's drive from the two-mile Cup venue. The track's marketing vice president, Pat Patterson, arranged for Stewart to drive a locally owned car in the week's Super Late Model feature. Stewart had raced the previous year in a Thanksgiving midget race at the brand-new facility and had been impressed. For the most part, Stewart had limited his local stock-car races to dirt tracks, which he preferred, but he agreed to make an exception in the case of Irwindale. The decision signaled the end of Stewart's February vow not to race on local tracks.

"Maybe it won't be so bad out here," he said optimistically just before he left the big track after Winston Cup practice. Climbing into an unfamiliar car, Stewart performed reasonably well at Irwindale. After starting 17th, he drove up through the pack to finish seventh. A bump from a local driver almost put Stewart into the wall, giving him a chance to demonstrate his skill to the small-track fans. His car lurched to the outside and lost several positions, but he managed to avoid what looked like a certain crash.

Meanwhile, his team continued to endure baffling qualifying problems. For the fourth consecutive week, he qualified outside the top 30, though his 32nd-place start prevented him from having to take another provisional starting position. Teammate Bobby Labonte, noted for his qualifying prowess, was in a similar slump. He started even worse than Stewart, 36th, at Fontana after also needing a provisional at Talladega.

No one was more mystified by the qualifying woes—which, by the way, seemed to have no effect on the teams' performances on race day—than Gibbs. "Our guys are normally great qualifiers," he said. "Other weeks we came away thinking maybe we knew what was wrong, but here we had problems that were really baffling. The good thing is that we have a good race setup, but I promise you, you don't want to start back there."

"This track is a lot like Michigan," Stewart said before the race.

"Las Vegas is sort of a track all its own. I'm not sure that it has the amount of banking that Michigan has; it's a flatter track than Michigan (the California Speedway turns are banked 14 degrees, as compared to 18 at Michigan Speedway), but the way you approach the weekend is pretty much the same as far as setups go. You just don't have the banking to help you like you do at Michigan."

California Speedway's detractors often refer to it as a cookie-cutter track, too similar to the other tracks Stewart noted. Though drivers generally like the track, some have suggested that it provides a blasé brand of racing, even comparing it to the multi-purpose baseball-football stadiums constructed in the 1960s and 1970s. They contend that the track is too flat for stock cars and too banked for Indy cars and that, as a result, it does not offer a high level of entertainment value for either.

"If a guy gets going and gets his car balanced, then he'll tend to run away," conceded Stewart. "That's just the characteristic of that kind of track. It's fast, it's flat, and momentum is so important there that if a guy is off just a little, he's off a lot. The drivers like it from the standpoint that if you can find a way to get around it a little better, then it'll help them in the long run. You end up racing the racetrack instead of each other."

Labonte finished second behind the Ford of Jeremy Mayfield, which made for quite a story in itself. Mayfield's 14th-place finish at Talladega had been tainted by NASCAR's discovery of a fuel additive—all of which are illegal. Harsh penalties would be announced two days after the California race. In fact, Mayfield's team was even punished after the California victory, when his Ford was found to be slightly lower than the required 51-inch roof height. Officials conceded that that the disparity could probably be explained by a dent Mayfield caused by jumping around on the roof in a joyous victory-lane celebration, but they fined the team anyway in a move that seemed petty and vengeful. The victory was allowed to stand, however.

The race was very nearly won by rookie Matt Kenseth, who dominated much of the contest but duplicated Rusty Wallace's Martinsville error by having four tires changed on his final pit stop and relinquishing track position he never regained.

"I had planned on losing all day," admitted the 28-year-old Kenseth. "I knew something was going to happen, and the minute I was thinking, 'Boy, are we in pretty good shape,' when I was hearing the lap times and everything else, and, sure enough, something happened."

Like Wallace, though, Kenseth absolved crew chief Robbie Reiser of any blame for the strategic blunder. "At the start of the day, I told Robbie to change four tires every time," Kenseth said. "Later on, I should have rethought that position. I don't have the experience to tell the difference between what will work on a long and short run (of green-flag racing). At the end, it took me a long time to get going."

Kenseth, by the way, did rally to finish third behind Mayfield and Labonte.

Labonte regained the season points lead, and never relinquished it over the remaining 24 races of the season.

Bad luck, which seemed to be in endless supply at the Home Depot team, struck Stewart yet again. On a green-flag pit stop, his Grand Prix skidded past his pit stall as it crossed a pool of oil left earlier by a blown engine in Elliott Sadler's Ford. Since Stewart's pit stall was near the pit entrance, a result of his poor starting position, he had to drive all the way down pit road at a snail's pace—NASCAR enforces speed limits for safety reasons—and take another lap around the track before finally pitting successfully. The mistake, which occurred under green-flag conditions, caused Stewart to fall to the back of all the cars racing on the lead lap, about 30th position.

Demonstrating just how strong his car actually was, Stewart rallied magnificently but reached only 10th place by the race's end.

"I really feel bad for Tony," said Gibbs. "I think, if that had not happened, he was probably going to win the race."

Stewart was inconsolable after the race and promptly pitched a tantrum that Gibbs grudgingly admired. "He is fun to work with, I'm telling you right now," said Gibbs later. "Yes, he'll blow up. I walked up to him after the race, and I'm going to congratulate him on finishing in the top 10, and when he saw me, he turned around and vented for about five minutes. He said, 'I'm sick and tired . . . ,' and he went off and chewed me out, half the people in our program out and everybody else, but I didn't get upset about that.

"I got excited about that because I know finishing 10th to him stunk. You don't want to finish 10th. He wants to win a race. I'm just trying to paint a little picture of what it's like working with him. To me, it's exciting."

Stewart's pilot, Bob Burris, has been with the young driver since his open-wheel days and probably spends as much time with him as anyone. Noting the growing discontent with Stewart's behavior, Burris staunchly defended him.

"He's the same guy he's always been," Burris said. "There isn't a thing wrong with Tony that a couple of victories wouldn't cure.

"Yeah, when things go bad for him, he can be a handful, but it's because he wants to win so bad, and that's the very reason he's so darn good at what he does. You could change him, you could lay down the law, but all you'd be doing was putting out that competitive fire, and I'm telling you, that's not something you want to do. Just leave him alone. Tony'll be all right."

It would get worse before it got better.

12

ROCK BOTTOM

RICHMOND, Virginia
May 2000

All of Tony Stewart's frustrations converged on a warm Saturday night at the very site of his most famous triumph. His first career victory had occurred at Richmond International Raceway on September 11, 1999, and when he arrived at the lightly-banked, three-quarter-mile track, Stewart was primed to win again.

Unlike Las Vegas and California, where Stewart might have won, this was the first night where he should have. He qualified seventh, putting the problems of the previous weeks behind. He performed flawlessly in the Pontiac Excitement 400. Nevertheless, the race ended up being the *piece de resistance* of what, to this point, was Tony Stewart's season of frustrations.

The race was a vintage Stewart performance. Patient early, he bided his time and communicated astutely with crew chief Greg Zipadelli, honing the handling characteristics necessary to produce victory. For most of the race, pole winner Rusty Wallace's Ford led. Wallace seemed superior on long runs—on fresh tires, his car was capable of pulling away. As long as caution flags occurred before Wallace was able to put fresh tires on, he was able to maintain his advantage, but when the action was not interspersed with yellow-flag periods to afford Wallace that convenience, Stewart came to the fore.

Stewart led 69 laps and would have led many more. By the race's closing stages, Wallace found himself buried deep in the pack, his four-tire pit stop resulting in the loss of track position when other drivers either failed to pit or changed two. For some reason, one which Wallace could not fully explain, he found himself unable to get his Taurus back to the front. His car simply appeared to be not as maneuverable as Stewart's in making its way through slower traffic on the ¾-mile, D-shaped track.

By the final pit stop, the race was Stewart's to win. He had clearly established his superiority. The pit crew expertly changed four tires for the final time at lap 338 and Stewart steamed back out, seemingly ahead of the other cars pitting.

The second-place car of Dale Earnhardt Jr. was pitting several stalls in front of Stewart's car. As Stewart drove by, Earnhardt Jr. turned radically left, his own path blocked by the still-stationary Ford of Kevin Lepage, and spun his wheels to tighten the turning radius. The nose of Earnhardt's Monte Carlo hit Stewart's car squarely in the fresh left-rear tire.

"Oh, Christ," Stewart blurted to his crew via his radio. "The damn tire's flat.

"I only saw him [Earnhardt Jr.] out of the corner of my eye," he said later, "then I realized I had a flat. . . . If it was in middle of race, it wouldn't have been an issue. It pretty much killed our chances. Greg [Zipadelli] was pretty much the calmest person there. 'You got 35 laps to go,' he said. 'Go after it, and get what you can.' It put my mind in positive light."

For the second time in as many weeks, Stewart had to drive all the way back around the track, this time with a flat tire, and pit again. For the purposes of winning the race, the night was over.

Without question, the contact had been unintentional. Hitting Stewart's car could just as easily damaged Earnhardt Jr.'s red Chevrolet beyond repair. As it was, the car suffered only minor damage. However, the incident could not have benefited Earnhardt Jr. any better had he enlisted a sniper to shoot out Stewart's tire. A few laps later, Earnhardt Jr. passed his father, who had taken the lead by passing up the opportunity to pit and thus had gambled by racing with worn tires on his own Chevrolet. The small aerodynamic disadvantage of having a slightly crumpled nose slowed Earnhardt Jr. down in the final laps, but he was able to cross the finish line just ahead of a fast-closing Terry Labonte, also driving a Chevrolet.

Stewart, once again duplicating his California performance, rallied to finish eighth after the pit-road incident had put him in 23rd place. The moment the race was over, however, his temper exploded. He drove too fast into the garage after the checkered flag fell, sending several bystanders dashing for cover, and made no secret of his fury as a trail of reporters approached him for comment.

Nothing Stewart said got him in trouble. He did not blame Earnhardt Jr. for the pit-road melee. "It's not his fault, it's not my fault, it's just racing," Stewart said. "I'm not angry."

He was angry, though, and he kicked at the foot of an ESPN cameraman blocking his path to the team's transporter. Then he disappeared inside.

Zipadelli did blame Earnhardt Jr. for the accident on pit road, though he controlled his own anger. "[Earnhardt Jr.] just pulled out," said Zipadelli calmly. "He blocked us, and it cost us a shot at the win.

Look at the tape. He pulls out, there's nobody here, and he pulls all the way out . . . That's what I call blocking.

"That's the way our season is going. We can't do anything right right now. With 30 to go, we're running away from him and thinking we're going to win it. We get a caution flag, or we don't. That's just the way this game is. Up, down, up down, or whatever. We've had good cars. We just haven't been able to close deals. Eighth-place finishes are starting to wear on me.

"It was racing. It's going to happen all the time. I guess we need to start racing that way. The hell with everybody else, take care of yourself."

Tony Eury, Earnhardt Jr.'s winning crew chief, countered by saying Stewart had not given his driver enough room to get out of the pits. Video replays lent little credence to either contention. There simply had not been enough room for the course the two cars took.

"That one incident I feel pretty bad about," Earnhardt Jr. said. "He really didn't give me a lot of room to get out there, and I hate that he cut his tire. He really had the best car here tonight. It's a shame for him and his crew."

Stewart's behavior toward reporters was the result of pure frustration. The losses were piling up. NASCAR officials called Stewart and Joe Gibbs into their mobile command center for post-race discussions.

Three days later, Stewart was apologetic for his actions. The following day, Gibbs said he had been embarrassed.

"I was really looking forward to Richmond," Stewart said. "Obviously, I wanted to win, but we're happy with Richmond. It was just bad luck. We ran well, and just the performance alone, how well we ran, gave us a lot of momentum."

"The hard thing, the bad thing about our sport, is this," Stewart added. "I was talking to a guy yesterday, and he talked about how, imagine if you're playing basketball . . . you don't have to answer how it makes you feel, not the second the game is over. They have that 10- or 20-minute cooling-off period where they're in the locker room or whatever, and then, once they've cooled off, they go talk about it.

"If I got out of my car and wasn't upset, I wouldn't be driving Winston Cup, and no one would want me in the race car. People deserve to see true emotion, I guess. If I can't give you an honest answer, if I can't act the way I really feel, and if I get in trouble for it, what's the use in answering the question?

"I was mad that I lost the race. I wasn't mad at Dale. I wasn't mad at anyone. The next day I went fishing. I was disappointed. The whole time I was fishing, I was trying to put a positive spin on what had happened. It was just racing luck. I haven't had any racing luck all year. We thought everything was going our way, and it wasn't."

In the aftermath of the furor surrounding the race, Stewart felt betrayed by reporters he had considered friends. He could not come to grips with the fact that his own actions and words had played a powerful role in his predicament.

"Lots of guys say you're a breath of fresh air," he said, hurt and embittered. "Five guys applaud it, but one guy just crucifies you. That's why drivers give cookie-cutter answers. It's a lot easier to give standard answers. Most of them would like to say the same things I say. Either their sponsor won't let them, or it's just responses to e-mail. You don't have to like me. If I get an honest question, I give an honest answer. Maybe one day I won't last long in this sport, but I'm going to be honest.

"It's one of those racing deals, I guess. The last time I checked, I was a race driver and not a politician. Only in the last year and a half did I feel any pressure to say certain things."

When Stewart went fishing on the Sunday after the race, he got sunburned.

13

"HE WANTS TO BE GREAT"

CONCORD, North Carolina
May 2000

Tony Stewart and his team could not have chosen a less desirable, higher-profile arena for their next race than The Winston, NASCAR's all-star showcase, at Lowe's Motor Speedway. The 1.5-mile track, known as Charlotte Motor Speedway until a home-improvement chain bought the naming rights, is the *de facto* center of the sport, even though NASCAR is officially headquartered in Daytona Beach, Florida. All but a few teams are situated within a half-hour's drive of the mammoth track, which seats more than 160,000. Charlotte events draw extraordinary media coverage. Most of the newspapers, magazines, television production companies, and public relations firms that either specialize in or emphasize stock car racing are located within driving distance of the track.

Reams of copy trailed Stewart following his Richmond race. Motorsports writers either chided him for losing his temper or vividly celebrated his candor. Some of the stories were complimentary, but the effect of all the media attention was to leave the team with a siege mentality. Stewart felt stung by the criticism and somewhat betrayed by journalists in whom he had confided. He either saw only the negative clippings, or they were the only ones that had a notable effect on him.

He talked about receiving hate mail and being unable to sleep at night. What was plainly obvious was that beneath Stewart's fiery, competitive spirit existed a truly sensitive individual.

Suddenly, the Martinsville fans who had boisterously cheered the previous year when he flew off the handle in the Kenny Irwin incident were nowhere to be seen. He was hearing from "concerned" parties with a stake in his career: sponsors, marketers, merchants of his souvenir products, and all the various forces whose interests are best served by athletes who always say and do "the right things."

Joe Gibbs, who once coached National Football League personalities as diverse and controversial as John Riggins, Joe Theismann, and Dexter Manley, came to his driver's defense in the week leading up to The Winston.

"First of all, everyone is different," Gibbs noted. "Some of the greatest competitors I've ever known were very quiet. Some showed little emotion but were great competitors. On the other hand, [wide receiver] Gary Clark would explode at the drop of a hat. That was something that wasn't faked. It was his genuine personality.

"In Tony's case, I am absolutely convinced that this guy has one of the best hearts of anyone I've ever been around. If he does make a mistake, he is one of the few who will go back, apologize, even write letters. He's put his whole life into being a race-car driver. He wants to be the best in the world at what he does. It is a thrill to go to the track with Tony Stewart. He gives it everything he's got. For me, I think Tony Stewart is great for racing. I think people like to see someone with that kind of competitiveness in him."

At the time, some were even calling for Gibbs to calm his young driver down. Others thought Gibbs would not put up with Stewart's mercurial behavior. Those observers were perhaps a bit unmindful of

Gibbs' past and his ability, shared by many natural leaders, to motivate persons of widely disparate personality types.

What Gibbs knew was that attempting to modify the behavior of an athlete off the field, track, or court sometimes has an adverse effect on his performance. Gibbs had no desire to rob Stewart of his soul.

"The point I go back to is this," Gibbs said. "If he was the wrong kind of person, or a jerk, I'd be the first person to stop him. I think he's going to go down in history as one of this sport's greatest competitors, and I think he's great for this sport. He's fun to work with, but, yes, he'll blow up, and, yes, he'll tell you what he thinks."

Once again, Gibbs brought up Stewart's post-race explosion in California. "He vented for five minutes and chewed out half the people in our program," Gibbs recalled. "That, to me, I got excited about that. Finishing 10th, to him, stunk. He didn't want to finish 10th. To me, that's exciting.

"Everybody who has that personal relationship with Tony knows him. . . . At different times, he has done things he gets upset about, wishes he hadn't done, and we wish he hadn't. In a lot of those, he's not going to make the same mistake again. He is always willing, the day after, he wants to come back, he wants to make amends for it. I'd be willing to bet you, if you asked the management team [of sponsor Home Depot], what do they think about Tony Stewart, I'd bet—and there are 220,000 people in their management team—I bet they'd say, we love Tony Stewart. He likes people. They like people. He does a good job representing himself, and he's a great person. As soon as things start going his way, you'll see him start walking away with some wins."

His team embattled, Stewart seemed confused, but Judy Dominick, his long-suffering aide, took almost everything harder than Stewart himself. She was a nervous wreck. The task of restoring some semblance of normality fell to crew chief Greg Zipadelli, a man who feels actions are far more important than words. Zipadelli strained to maintain his calming influence on Stewart.

"Uh, yeah, I mean, I enjoy challenges like that," said Zipadelli, "and that [keeping Stewart on an even keel] is a good one. He [Stewart] has helped me mature as a person, and maybe as a leader, in adjusting to those situations.

"It's hard to read a person's mind. He'll pay the price, and he's more than willing to accept the consequences the next day. You can't ask more than that out of a person. This sport is emotional. You put in a lot of time and emotion. It's hard to control your emotions. On the positive side, that's what makes Tony such a passionate person. People don't want to look past what he just said. Well, that's my answer to that: he's a winner. He's not a good loser. That's what makes him special. He's not a lot of fun in tough moments, but that's what this sport is all about."

Gibbs knew that maturity would come with time. He empathized with Stewart's difficulties in adjusting to the responsibilities that accompany stardom.

"Most people who start in life, they picture things one way, and they want to be a success, they want to be a star," Gibbs observed. "Sometimes they don't realize what goes with that. You don't have a time to slip off and be by yourself. Many times, it seems like you belong to the fans.

"When I coached the Redskins, I was Washington's coach. I was the people's coach. I had to learn to live with that. Tony doesn't like that; he likes to get away by himself. On the other hand, he wants to be a success. He wants to be great. You're not going to reach greatness;

you're not going to make the money, without having a lot of other things, without having the down side of it to contend with. A lot of people, if placed in similar circumstances, would say, 'I'm sick and tired of this.'

"But let me tell you something else about Tony. He loves the fans. He loves to see them wearing his T-shirts. He reads his press clippings. Yet, and I think this shows what kind of person he is, all in all, I don't read a lot of negative stuff about him. There's some negative stuff, sure. I think he is hurt by it. He wants people to like him. He wants to be what everybody thinks he should be, but he also thinks it's important to be what he is. It hurts him sometimes, when someone writes something [negative], or it could be a fan who calls him names. He does care. . . . I don't think Tony can blow it off. It bothers him."

The Winston kicked off what basically was a two-week festival of speed at Lowe's Motor Speedway. May is the height of auto racing in the United States. While Charlotte was hosting The Winston and then NASCAR's longest race, the Coca-Cola 600, on consecutive weekends, the Midwest played home to practice and qualifying for the Indianapolis 500. Stewart, of course, was shuttling back and forth between the two cities. He was probably thankful at having so much to occupy his time and keep his mind off his problems.

The month was unusually tumultuous for reasons that made Stewart's unrest seem insignificant. During the previous week, when Winston Cup teams were enjoying an open date, Adam Petty had been killed in a Busch Grand National practice crash in New Hampshire. When 19-year-old Petty had made his Cup debut at Texas on April 2, he became the fourth generation of NASCAR's most prominent family to compete at its highest level. His death had a profound effect on the sport.

The all-star race in Charlotte would prove to be another of Dale Earnhardt Jr.'s nights. It had taken Stewart 25 races to collect the first of his three victories in 1999, his rookie season. Now, the 25-year-old Earnhardt had won his 12th and 16th starts and then followed up with another victory the next week in the The Winston (though it did not count, officially, because NASCAR awards no points to the all-star race's participants). The Winston was run on Stewart's 29th birthday.

The Winston's unusual format consists of three segments—30, 30, and 10 laps, respectively—with the winner of the final segment being declared the winner. Pole winner Bill Elliott won the first and second segments. Stewart was nominally competitive, finishing 10th in the first segment. On the 24th lap of the second segment, however, he was in a furious battle for seventh place with Ward Burton and Mark Martin when his Pontiac bumped Martin's Ford on the back stretch. The incident drew a chorus of boos when Martin's car slammed hard into the concrete wall on the outside of the track.

"What happened was I didn't think Mark would come down that low," said Stewart via radio to his pit crew. "He went to block me, and I was already down there. I didn't mean to do it."

Martin, who has a justly deserved reputation as being a clean driver, was charitable in his account. "I'm not sure what happened," he said. "I was holding somebody up, I guess. If I had been fast enough, nobody could have caught up with me to bump me."

Stewart, who had finished second in the race the previous year, wound up 15th in the final standings.

In the final segment, Earnhardt Jr. used drafting help from his father to pass reigning Winston Cup champion Dale Jarrett on the back stretch with two laps to go. The victory earned him $515,000. As it turned out, Earnhardt Jr. would stagger through the final 21 races of the season without so much as a top-10 finish, but on the heels of his Winston victory, he seemed likely to supplant Stewart as the most successful rookie in the history of the sport.

"It's kind of funny for me to stand there on that podium and hear people cheering, 'Earnhardt! Earnhardt! Earnhardt!' when I'm the only Earnhardt standing up there," he said after the race. "I made sure the 'big Earnhardt' hurried up and got up there so I didn't feel so weird anymore. He's the 'Earnhardt' in the family, and he's the reason the fans are cheering Earnhardt."

A tragedy occurred after the race. At practically the same time Earnhardt Jr. was basking in the glow of his dramatic victory, a pedestrian bridge located behind the main grandstands, built to facilitate passage across U.S. Highway 29, collapsed as fans were rushing to the parking lots. Miraculously, no one was killed, but dozens were injured, and by the time Earnhardt Jr. arrived in the press box to discuss his performance, many of the journalists had departed to cover the late-night disaster.

14

EVERYONE BUT TONY

CONCORD, North Carolina
May 2000

In the next week leading up to NASCAR's longest race, the Coca-Cola 600, the racing world turned its attention to the extraordinary exploits of the Second Coming of Dale. One writer speculated that the 25-year-old rookie's birth had been accompanied by the arrival of "three moonshiners bearing gifts."

Stewart, meanwhile, immersed himself in his dual roles as NASCAR driver and Indianapolis 500 race-car owner. On the day after The Winston, the roles became a bit confused. The 500's final day of qualifying, held one week before the world's most famous race, is known as Bubble Day. No provisional starts are awarded—the field consists of only the 33 fastest cars. If, during the final qualifying session, the lowest driver on the totem pole is bested by another driver's time, he's out. The 33rd qualifier in the ever-changing rankings is thus referred to as being "on the bubble."

No, Stewart did not actually compete in the Indianapolis 500, as he had in 1999, but he didn't exactly step aside, either. His team entered two cars in the race. When Dr. Jack Miller was unable to produce a qualifying time, Stewart intervened. He climbed into the car, took it out for practice, adjusted the setup, and ran laps considerably faster than the driver he had hired. Then he turned the car back over to Miller, who made another four-lap qualifying attempt, slipped out of the racing groove, and still failed to make the field.

Back in Charlotte Dale Earnhardt Jr. was having a happier time. In a downtown parade, part of the Speed Street festival, crowds greeted Earnhardt Jr. so warmly that ticker tape seemed conspicuous by its absence. "Sometimes, it's overwhelming," said NASCAR's new kid on the block. "It's always, to a point, overwhelming. Failure, too. . . . Sometimes you can't believe what's happening. I get in a little mode when I'm at the racetrack where I'm focusing on a race car. I don't pay attention to a whole lot else. We get to the house and kick back on the couch, sit in an air-conditioned room, and drink beer." Young Earnhardt's sponsor, by the way, is Budweiser.

Like Stewart, he is a breath of fresh air, but the two have little in common. Stewart is obsessed with racing and has little interest in anything else. Earnhardt Jr. is a more apt spokesman for his generation, less inhibited than most of his peers and unafraid to confess freely to a love of alternative-rock music and beer. He seems to have even less in common with his fierce, intractable father than with Stewart, though.

In the midst of the "Little E" euphoria, things got weird for Tony Stewart. Behind the scenes, he continued to feel pressure from the furor caused by his Richmond remarks. Stewart became quite deeply affected by the public response to his outspokenness. He felt that the full story had not been told: His reasonable, honest comments on the price of fame and fortune had been misconstrued to make him appear petty and unappreciative. Stewart decided—or consented—to hold a press conference in which he apologized for his actions. The conference was convened hastily in the Lowe's Motor Speedway infield media center. Joe Gibbs accompanied Stewart.

"Lots of rumors have been flying," said Stewart. "Am I happy? Absolutely. Am I frustrated? Yes. Have I got a lot to learn about how to conduct myself? Yes."

Somehow, Stewart had become the bad guy, and it was not a role he enjoyed. By saying he felt smothered at times, he had created an impression he had failed to anticipate. "One of the reasons I wanted to come in here and set the record straight is this," Stewart said, his voice painfully quiet. "I do love the fans. I don't want people to think that Tony Stewart does not like the fans. I'm not against fans having a chance to see their favorite drivers in the garage area. It's crowded sometimes, yes, but it's frustrating mainly because I'm not used to it.

"What's been difficult for me have been the times when I've signed autographs and greeted fans, but then, when I've had to do something else, it's been frustrating when people haven't understood that it's impossible to please everybody and handle all their requests. I don't have a lot of time, and I've got to spend part of that time with the guy who adjusts the shocks, part of it with my crew chief, part of it handling interviews, and there's just not enough time in the day."

Stewart also addressed rumors that he was considering going back to Indy cars or leaving the Gibbs team. "I don't plan on going anywhere," he said. "I'd be the first to admit I've got a temper. There's a fire in me that would char-broil a brontosaurus burger."

Gibbs understood the media. He was an old hand at recognizing the proper tone to take. He instinctively nudged Stewart, standing next to him, a bit farther than the driver was himself willing to go.

"We're not disputing that Tony said any of the things he was quoted as saying," said Gibbs. "We all know there have been a number of articles. He just wanted to come in here so that you could get the whole picture."

The press conference created the impression, rightly or wrongly, that Stewart was knuckling under, perhaps even selling out. The great majority of reporters present had not been critical of Stewart. Many valued him for his candor and many were unaware of problems in the Stewart camp. Afterward, common reaction to the press conference was, "What was that all about?"

Two nights later, Stewart encountered a sportswriter on the steps of the press box behind Lowe's Motor Speedway's new dirt track, where a World of Outlaws sprint-car race had just taken place. Stewart asked the writer what he thought of the press conference.

"I thought it was sad," the writer replied. Stewart didn't follow. "When you were a kid," the writer said, "did you ever have a hero in your hometown, a guy who always stood up for what was right and didn't take 'nothin' off nobody'? Then that day comes when your hero gets beaten down and he has to knuckle down to the boss, or the coach, or the principal, just like everybody else. That's what it felt like to me."

Stewart shrugged and walked down the steps, carrying with him a look of brooding sadness.

The whole situation had gotten completely out of hand, and perhaps it was inevitable. The greatest rookie in NASCAR history had found himself squarely in the middle of a sophomore jinx. Stewart won two out of the last three races of the 1999 season, and now it was the 12th race of 2000, and the new superstar was winless. Unquestionably, many of his wounds were self-inflicted, but what Stewart needed more than anything else was a victory. Not only had he failed to win; he had suffered excruciating losses.

The victory would not come in the Coca-Cola 600, where Stewart was one of five drivers eligible for Winston's No Bull Five bonus of $1 million. The eligible drivers were the top five finishers in Vegas:

Jeff Burton, Stewart, Mark Martin, Bill Elliott, and Bobby Labonte. Only Labonte came close. The race was delayed for more than an hour by rain and did not end until after 11 p.m. Stewart had qualified ninth and led two early laps, but by the marathon race's end, he was a lap off the pace and in 14th place.

A rookie won, but it was not the rookie everyone expected. Dale Earnhardt Jr., who had won the pole and set a track record (186.034 miles per hour), led 47 of the first 49 laps. However, the Coca-Cola 600 often goes to a driver who emerges in the late stages. Matt Kenseth, a 28-year-old protégé of Mark Martin from Cambridge, Wisconsin, never led until the 311th of 400 laps and then only for six laps, but he came back to pass Labonte with 26 laps remaining and eventually won by .573 of a second.

Now Kenseth was the second rookie winner of the season. Earnhardt Jr. finished fourth behind Kenseth, Labonte, and his father. "I don't have a nightclub in my basement, and Budweiser is not my sponsor," said Kenseth, in jest. "Dale Jr. and I enjoy some of the same things, but he still has a little more kid in him than I do, I guess."

If Stewart was out of control that season, then he only mirrored NASCAR as a whole. It seemed as if virtually anyone could win, and almost everyone had: Dale Jarrett, Bobby Labonte, Jeff and Ward Burton, Dale Earnhardt father and son, Rusty Wallace, Mark Martin, Jeff Gordon, Jeremy Mayfield, and now even Kenseth.

Almost everyone had won except Tony Stewart.

15

VICTORY AT LAST

DOVER, Delaware
June 2000

Joe Gibbs's two teams were headed in opposite directions in the standings. Bobby Labonte was ranked first in the Winston Cup point standings. Tony Stewart was in 10th place. Based on the final standings of the 1999 season, Labonte had risen a position, from second to first, but Stewart had fallen six positions, from fourth to 10th. All three of Stewart's top-five finishes in 2000 had occurred in the season's first five races. He had failed to complete three of the first 12.

"On Tony's side," said Gibbs, "it seems like the dream season he had as a rookie, the unbelievable fortune, has gone the other way. I will say this, and I honestly believe it. I go the track every week expecting the '20' car [Stewart's] to win every single race. That's how good I think Tony is, the team is, Greg [Zipadelli] is. There is not a track out there he can't win on.

"The way I think is, honestly, he's going to get five wins before the season is over."

Dover Downs International Speedway is one of those tracks that was built before architects got involved and before there were palatial modern facilities for new tracks to use as models. Dover is an oval built just outside another. The inner oval was used to race horses, and

Tony Stewart streaking toward his first victory of the season at the MBNA 400 at Dover, Delaware, in June 2000. Tom Whitmore

originally the NASCAR track was simply a way to occupy the real estate and keep up the cash flow.

By 2000, however, stock car racing had far outstripped harness racing as the money producer for Dover Downs Entertainment. In fact, a slot casino had been built behind the enclosed grandstands on the NASCAR track's back stretch, and gaming had also become a more significant source of revenue than harness racing. For Winston Cup races, the mile track drew more than 100,000 fans, and plans were being made to build an on-site hotel and to increase seating to more than 170,000. The track is now paved in concrete, a more durable surface.

Dover has unusually steep banking in its turns—24 degrees—for a relatively short track. Located only 10 miles or so from Delaware Bay, the track also tends to be quite hot in June. These two factors help make the MBNA Platinum 400 a stern test of conditioning as well as driving ability.

"The biggest thing is that you're in the corners for so long, and you run so fast here," Stewart said. "It just keeps putting a lot of load on your body. That's why Dover is such a physically demanding race."

Another driver, Ken Schrader, put it this way. "The 600 miles we just ran at Charlotte doesn't compare to the 400 miles we run at Dover," he said. "If you aren't having a good run, Dover makes for a long day. It is a very demanding track. . . . Just one little slip, and the track will jump up and bite you."

"One of the biggest things at Dover is not abusing your tires," noted Jimmy Makar, Labonte's crew chief. "It seems like you can go fast with almost any [chassis] setup, but some setups abuse the tires more than others. So you have to work hard with your setup to be sure that you'll be able to conserve the tires. It's a real balancing act.

"Dover is a place where you can get 'swept up' into trouble easily. It's a narrow, fast racetrack. There's not a lot of room to maneuver around trouble in front of you. You have to be able to 'race the track' instead of other cars all day long. As far as handling characteristics of the car, the car needs to turn well in the center of the corner [at each end of the track] and not be loose [unstable] coming off the corner. That's typically what people fight here."

Ford driver Rusty Wallace was the fastest qualifier, turning a lap at an average speed of 157.411 mph. Stewart qualified a respectable, if not particularly impressive, 16th.

Stewart and Zipadelli seldom concentrate on qualifying, though. "What you do for qualifying is totally different from what you do in the race," Stewart said. "Basically, a lot of cars qualify down at the bottom of the track [in the turns], but, by the time you're about 40 or

50 laps into the race, there are cars all the way from the bottom of the track to right against the outside wall. That's a big difference in between.

"Basically, everybody just searches around on the racetrack for the spot that makes his car happy. Obviously, I'm going to make my Pontiac as happy as possible."

That Stewart did. To borrow a line used in a newspaper account of the race, he "finally went so fast that not even bad luck could beat him."

Stewart took the lead for the first time on the 72nd lap, and by lap 107, he was ready to establish superiority. By lap 292, when Stewart pitted, his pursuers had changed their strategies. If the race were completed under green-flag conditions, Stewart would have to pit again, so practically all of the other contenders slowed down, hoping to beat Stewart by conserving fuel.

Zipadelli faced the unavoidable reality that Stewart could not, under any circumstances, make it to the checkered flag without pitting again. Stewart had lost a race under similar circumstances in New Hampshire the previous season, so Zipadelli instructed Stewart to keep driving hard in hopes that he could stretch his lead so far that he'd be able to pit for a quick splash of gasoline and still keep the lead.

"I kind of thought we were going to save fuel," Stewart recalled later. "Then, all of a sudden, Greg comes on my radio and says, 'Take off.' At that point, I pulled the plug. I knew I was going to have to pit then, but I was trying to build up so big a lead that I could pit and no one would still be able to catch me."

As it turned out, fuel economy became a moot issue. Two caution periods occurred late in the race, the first at lap 382 when Jeff Gordon's Chevrolet bounced off the wall in turn four, and another at lap 391 when Sterling Marlin's Chevy hit the inside wall on the front straight

Stewart enthusiastically celebrates his long over-due victory at Dover.
Tom Whitmore

after a tap from behind by Kyle Petty's Pontiac. Stewart pitted, as did everyone else, at which point all the mechanics could dispense with their calculators and shut down their laptop computers.

Matt Kenseth, coming off his surprising victory the week before, drove the only car capable of competing with Stewart's. However, Kenseth's mechanics, trying perhaps too hard to improve their car, made an adjustment that backfired on the last stop.

"At the end, I had them make the car too tight [difficult to turn],

Stewart (left) poses for a victory photo at Dover with team owner Joe Gibbs, Tessa Goetz, and Lori Lundgren. Tom Whitmore

and that was my fault," Kenseth said. "I think I could have run with him [Stewart]. I don't know that I could have beaten him."

"I knew he [Kenseth] had a good run," said Stewart. "My car was best after probably 20 or 25 laps. . . . I think Matt's car was a little better right off the get-go [on fresh tires], but I got about three or four laps on [new] tires, it seemed like it evened out, and I started pulling away once again."

Stewart's blistering pace left only five cars on the lead lap at the end. Stewart's teammate, Labonte, who kept Kenseth occupied defending second place in the final handful of laps, finished third, and the Ford teammates Dale Jarrett and Ricky Rudd also completed the full distance.

Just as significant to Stewart as his day's earnings, $152,830, was a thunderous and warm reception from the massive crowd. Coming on the heels of two weeks of boos in Charlotte, basking in the glory did much to heal Stewart's bruised ego.

"That was very nice," he said. "That's much better, to me, than the money and the trophy, knowing I have people who support me. Driving around the track [as his car slowed after taking the checkered flag], I could see the fans cheering. I wish I had words to express it. It's a nice feeling to see the people want to see us win."

After the race, however, Stewart made yet another misstep in his already stormy dealings with the media. In victory lane, during radio and television interviews, Stewart seemed to contradict his Charlotte declaration that he had not been misquoted. It was an almost inadvertent slip, due in no small part to the fact that he was excited after the long-awaited victory. Stewart made reference to "some things that I said and some that I didn't say."

Instantly, a handful of reporters cried foul. One even called the Dover Downs infield media center from his home in North Carolina and asked another reporter to ask Stewart to clarify his remark.

Stewart had just completed his press-box session when the question arrived from the infield. Dover public relations director John Dunlap relayed it: "Ask Tony if he is saying that he has been misquoted by reporters."

Stewart could have left the question unanswered. He should have left the question unanswered. Instead, he stopped, turned around, and took the microphone from Dunlap. Mike Arning, his public-relations representative, wore a blank stare as Stewart passed up an opportunity to back away from what, in victory lane, had been a fairly harmless and oblique reference.

"Yes," Stewart said, "some of the things that were printed were things that I did not say. They presented only one side of the story.

Yes, I have a difficult time when fans ask for autographs in the garage area, especially when I am talking with my crew or trying to concentrate on the task at hand, but everyone who knows me also knows that I love my fans, and that I would do anything for them."

At the very least, Stewart was blurring the line between claiming that his remarks were taken out of context and actually alleging that quotes had been made up. In point of fact, he was wrong. His Richmond remarks had been tape-recorded by dozens of writers, and he had not been misquoted. By saying that he had been, he was questioning the ethics, and not merely the judgment, of the handful of journalists who had written the stories Stewart found to be offensive. To a man, they were infuriated, and not without justification. Stewart did not understand how serious such matters are to journalists.

To Stewart, the moment was a negligible footnote of a triumphant day, and when he was subsequently criticized, he once again felt as if several journalists were out to get him. He did not fully grasp the import of alleging that a journalist was making up quotes. From his perspective, the most important remark had been his contention that he did not hate the fans and that his positions had been incompletely depicted. From the journalists' perspective, Stewart was now calling them liars.

16

ONE MORE TIME

BROOKLYN, Michigan
June 2000

Tony Stewart really turned the corner on his season at Michigan Speedway. Not only did he win the Kmart 400 on June 11, but he also won a public-relations victory. Many drivers admired Stewart for his willingness to speak out, and it was no small help to Stewart when one of the more respected competitors in the Winston Cup offered his support.

Stewart had inadvertently bumped Mark Martin's car during The Winston, yet Martin was sympathetic and compassionate in his remarks to the media. "I understand what [Stewart's] going through," Martin said. "I think everybody in the garage understands what he's going through. I went through the same thing.

"It was overwhelming for me in 1990. I almost drowned. We ran for the championship with [Dale] Earnhardt, and it was big. And it was very intense, and it was a dramatic experience for my family and me to go through, and since then nothing's been quite the same."

Martin, 41, was the ultimate veteran of the Winston Cup wars. For 11 years in a row, Martin had finished sixth or better in the point standings without once winning a championship. Three times—in

1990, 1994, and 1998—Martin had finished second. His Martinsville victory on April 9 had been the 32nd of his career.

Martin understood Stewart's difficulty adjusting to the presence of hundreds of fans in the garage area, all vying for autographs while the driver tried to prepare for races. "You know, it's a tough situation," Martin said. "For years and years, I raced and, after every race, I stood by the race car and signed autographs while the team loaded everything up. They let the whole grandstands come down into the pits, and I signed autographs for everybody who wanted one. You can't do that anymore. That's when I raced at Springfield, Missouri, and places like that in ASA [American Speed Association] and stuff like that, back then. That's when maybe 3,000 people would be there that night. Now we have 3,000 people in the garage.

"Times have changed, racing has changed, and we can't service everybody . . . and, so, that's frustrating for the fans, and it's frustrating for the drivers because, no matter what we do, we can't do enough. That frustrates us, and it frustrates them, too, because they probably remember when [it was different]. They say things are changing, and they are. It's not that we don't want to; it's that we can't. When you've got 30 seconds, and you look at 100 people standing there, what do you do? Do you do one? Do you do 10? Or do you just do none? I mean, you don't have a good choice left in situations like that. I don't know what to do. Sometimes I just do the kids. Sometimes I can't even do that. Sometimes I do the kids, and the adults swear at me. You can't win. It's physically impossible for us to do the exact right thing."

Martin's comments were hardly different from what Stewart had said at Richmond, but Martin was a veteran, and the words carried greater authority. Stewart's youth worked against him. His wasn't as familiar a face to the fans as a Martin, an Earnhardt, or an Elliott. Jeff Gordon had never said anything nearly as controversial as Stewart, but

Gordon also had been booed even as he was winning three championships and 50 races over an eight-year period.

"Anybody who thinks being a race driver is an easy job ought to
try it sometime," said Stewart. "When I came down [south] and moved
to Cornelius [North Carolina], I thought I knew what was going to
happen. It was a big change for me. We all have to make adjustments
in our lives, not just race drivers, but anybody: when you move out of
your parents' house, when you're on your own for the first time.

"Well, I had a lot bigger adjustment to make than I thought. The
lifestyle, the demands on your time, the public pressure . . . sometimes
it gets overwhelming."

People were starting to get it, perhaps because the Dover victory
had exerted a calming influence on Stewart. The burning desire had
been fed. Stewart's tone had softened. He did not seem quite as much
the angry young man.

For all his frustrations with the demands on his time, Stewart thrives
on a busy schedule, so long as it's activity of his own choosing. During
the week leading up to the Kmart 400, Stewart visited fellow driver
Ken Schrader's dirt track in Peavley, Missouri, and tried his hand at
winged sprint cars. Stewart had previously driven the non-winged open-
wheel cars sanctioned by the United States Auto Club, and he did not
feel comfortable driving the winged cars, which have significantly
greater down force in the turns. Afterward, he compared notes with
Winston Cup rookie Dave Blaney, who had been a winged sprint-car
champion in the Pennzoil World of Outlaws circuit, though at Peavley,
Blaney turned his car over to another driver after competing in a heat
race. Joe Gibbs would have been proud.

On the Friday night prior to the Michigan race, Bob Burris piloted
Stewart's plane to Bristol, where the NASCAR oval had been coated
with dirt to facilitate World of Outlaws racing. "This was really some-

Stewart and team members celebrate their second victory in a row at the Kmart 400 at Michigan Speedway. Front row (left to right) Jason Shapiro, Jay Berry, Alan Copeland, and Gerald Shires. Back row Tessa Goetz, Greg "Zippy" Zipadelli, Stewart, Renee Perks, and Chris Woodward. Tom Whitmore

thing historic, something I wanted to see for myself," Stewart said. On Saturday night, Burris made the round-trip flight again with a group of Stewart cronies, but this time Stewart remained in Michigan to get a good night's sleep before the Sunday Cup race.

In Michigan qualifying, Bobby Labonte won the pole at a record 189.883 miles per hour, but the speed of his Pontiac wasn't matched by teammate Stewart, whose own speed, 186.099, forced him to start 28th.

"There are a lot of variables that go into a race team," Labonte noted. "Nobody planned it that way when we got here. Tony was a lot faster than I was at Dover, and there's nothing we [Labonte's team] could do about it there."

What Stewart proved quickly in the Michigan race was that his qualifying speed had little effect on his race performance. (Actually, he had not qualified particularly well at Dover, either.) Rain shortened the Kmart 400 by six laps, and Stewart, who had lost a rain-shortened race to Jeff Burton in Las Vegas, benefited from the precipitation this time.

The victory was incomplete, not undeserved. By the end, Stewart had demonstrated the superiority of his car over those driven by three more experienced pursuers: Dale Earnhardt, Labonte, and Dale Jarrett. When a caution flag waved eight laps from the scheduled end—Kenny Irwin's Chevrolet suffered engine failure, and the cars of Geoffrey Bodine and Robby Gordon tangled when they skidded through oil dropped by Irwin's car—it seemed as if the also-rans might get one more chance. Rain began pelting the track, however, and a red flag stopped the race at 196 laps.

Stewart admitted the sight of Earnhardt in his rear-view mirror had been a bit unnerving. "I knew the 18 [teammate Labonte] was not going to hurt me," Stewart said. "He may go by me, but the 3 [Earnhardt] wouldn't have had a problem roughing me up a little bit on the way by, just to say, 'hi.' He [Earnhardt] would've smiled and laughed as he was doing it. I didn't really like seeing [Earnhardt] back there at the end."

Earnhardt said Stewart had nothing to worry about. "I felt good that I was able to hold off Labonte for second," he said. "I think this was just meant to be a Pontiac day even if the rain *had* stayed away."

"When the yellow [flag] comes out, Earnhardt is the master," Stewart said. "He's always been good on restarts and good at doing what needs to be done. I wasn't sure I knew everything I needed to know at this racetrack to know exactly what to do with him there.

"I was prepared for it. I wasn't going to give it to him, by any means. I felt like I had a good enough car that, if I could make the first lap and get through those first two sets of corners, I'd have had a shot of getting through and getting away from him again."

Stewart found the victory somewhat unsatisfying due to the premature ending. "I'm happy winning two in a row," he said, "but is it an automatic cure [to my season]? No. I'm encouraged about the rest of the season, but we've got to race hard every week."

"It's kind of like Winston Cup every week," said Joe Gibbs. "Something different can happen to you, and I think for the first part of our season, for the 20 car [Stewart], it seemed like everything did. I thought we had a win at Richmond and a couple other places. We're running well, and that's important. If you hang in there long enough, usually the bad breaks will even themselves out."

Spoken like a true coach.

"You always feel bad on a deal like this [premature ending]," Gibbs added. "You'd like to win it racing on the track. I will say this: [bad luck] has certainly happened to us a bunch. In any case, you take what you can get, and [this time] it kind of went our way with the rain."

17

MAN BITES DOG

LONG POND, Pennsylvania
June 2000

C ould Tony Stewart win three races in a row? Was this the same driver who seemed so utterly demoralized and embattled as recently as the May 28 Coca-Cola 600 at Lowe's Motor Speedway?

By the time the Winston Cup circuit arrived in the Pocono Mountains of northwestern Pennsylvania for the first of two visits, Stewart had regained the form of his superlative rookie season. It was as if the diversions of May had vanished into thin air. His many fans could justifiably say, "I told you so." There had been nothing wrong with Stewart that a couple of victories could not cure.

"There never was anything wrong with Tony," said Bob Burris, the driver's pilot and friend. "The Tony Stewart that I've known for years is absolutely unchanged. When he and I are on the plane, just talking about things, you couldn't ask for a better guy. He just wants to win. He wants that more than anything in the world. That's why he gets upset when things are going bad. If he didn't pitch a fit every now and then, odds are things wouldn't get better. The people around him know he wants to win, and it rubs off on them."

Ronny Crooks, the team's shock specialist, agreed. "To tell you the truth, I kind of like it when Tony blows off some steam," Crooks said.

"That makes me know he is committed to winning. Some of these guys, if you listen to them on the radio, when there are 20 laps to go, they're talking about how they're going to get out of the racetrack and beat the traffic. It doesn't matter if Tony's leading or if he's 50 laps down, he's still out there trying to pick up positions and beat somebody.

"I've worked with a lot of guys in this business over the years, and every one of them, at least the ones who were great drivers, hated to lose. When Tony gets out of that car and throws something, or stomps off into the transporter, that lets me know he wants it [victory] as bad as anybody."

Stewart very nearly won the Pocono 500, a fact that was obscured by the race's dramatic finish. Rusty Wallace won his fifth pole of the season, setting a record with a lap around the 2.5-mile, triangular track at 171.625 miles per hour. Fords took the first three positions. Stewart's lap, 170.581 miles per hour, was the fastest by a Pontiac driver but only ninth best overall.

Pocono Raceway is an unusual track. It is as long as Daytona or Indianapolis, but it has an odd triangular shape. The three straights are all of different lengths, and each of the turns that connect them is banked differently. The front straight is 3,740 feet long; the first turn is banked 14 degrees. The second straight is 3,055 feet; the second turn is banked 8 degrees. The third straight is a mere 1,780 feet; the third turn is banked 6 degrees. Pocono is the only "oval"—in auto racing parlance, any track is an oval if it requires only left turns—in which drivers shift gears each lap. The number of gear shifts varies from driver to driver.

Naturally, this kind of challenge appealed to Stewart. "I like it because it has the three turns, and they're all different," he said. "All three have different personalities. If you get the car good in one corner, sometimes it's bad in one of the others, and yet tolerable somewhere else. The challenge is getting the car to handle through all three corners all day."

Stewart said he used his shift lever "because my motor man tells me that's the only way to go fast here. Everybody shifts here."

Rain forced postponement of the race from Sunday, June 18, to Monday, June 19. The following week's race was all the way across the country in the Napa Valley north of San Francisco at Sears Point Raceway, a road course. A day lost at Pocono only worsened an already hectic journey; team transporters would have to make the long drive to the West Coast by alternating drivers around the clock. When Monday morning dawned clear at Pocono, mechanics were already gritting their teeth in preparation for Sears Point.

Until an inopportune yellow flag with 17 laps to go, Stewart was well on his way to a third consecutive victory. When he pitted at that point, the crew changed only right-side tires, and for once that was the strategy followed by almost everyone. However, Stewart entered the pits in the lead and exited them behind the Chevrolet of Dale Earnhardt and the Fords of Jeremy Mayfield and Dale Jarrett.

"I stalled the car, basically, getting ready to leave [the pits]," Stewart said. "After that, I had a hard time getting through traffic."

Though Stewart chose not to discuss it, he was reportedly angry at fellow Pontiac driver John Andretti, whose car was a lap down. Andretti's fierce battle with Stewart enabled the drivers in front of him to escape, and he wound up in sixth place, two positions worse than when he completed his pit stop.

The small controversy between Stewart and Andretti ended up being only a footnote to a race that featured intense drama on the final lap. Mayfield, whose first career victory had occurred at Pocono on June 21, 1998, pulled quite a surprise, engineering what journalists are fond of calling a "man bites dog" story. Somehow Mayfield's Ford made up perhaps six to eight car lengths on Earnhardt's Chevy in the first two turns of the final lap. When the two cars steamed through the final turn, Mayfield was right on Earnhardt's bumper. In fact, the two cars touched. Mayfield nudged Earnhardt, whose car wobbled and slipped perilously close to the wall. Not only did Mayfield win, but two other Ford drivers, teammates Jarrett and Ricky Rudd, also slipped past Earnhardt to give the Tauruses a 1-2-3 finish.

Earnhardt, who made a career out of similarly aggressive tactics, could hardly complain, and to his credit, he did not. "I reckon I slowed down a little," Earnhardt said, tension dripping from every syllable as he briefly held court in the garage. "I got beat. It was good racing."

Mayfield, a happy-go-lucky Kentuckian, could barely contain himself. In the days following the race, Earnhardt did grow weary at what he perceived as Mayfield's crowing about the victory.

"If you've watched a lot of Cup races, you've got to know what I was thinking," said Mayfield. "If you pass [Earnhardt] in turn one, he's going to get you back and get you loose. He's done it to me *a lot*, and that's probably why there weren't a lot of other drivers taking up for him.

"A lot of people talk about Earnhardt coming up the hard way and being a hard racer. Well, so am I. If he comes back after me, I'll go right back after him."

No one could remember the great Earnhardt being on the receiving end of such a comeuppance. The finish was gloriously dramatic.

"I don't think I can ever top that as far as winning a race goes," said Mayfield. "[Earnhardt] knows what happened. To his credit, he didn't make excuses or start talking about it. You've never heard me say anything when I've lost, either. That's just the way racing is."

Even Stewart, who reveres Earnhardt, smiled about the incident. "You've seen how Earnhardt is," he said, a twinkle in his eyes. "I mean, it's hard to say he didn't have it coming."

18

UNDER THE WEATHER

SONOMA, California
June 2000

nother testimony to Tony Stewart's innate talent is the ease with which he adapts to road racing. Prior to his switch to NASCAR, he had not raced on road courses since the go-kart days of his early teens. Sprint cars, midgets, and Silver Crown cars race exclusively on ovals, as do the rear-engined cars of the Indy Racing League.

Yet Stewart excelled immediately on the two road-racing venues of the Winston Cup Series: Sears Point Raceway in Sonoma, California, and Watkins Glen International, in upstate New York. In his rookie season, Stewart had qualified second at Sears Point, then gone on to finish a respectable 15th; at Watkins Glen, he had qualified fourth and finished sixth.

"I raced on road courses in go-karts when I was younger, so I've driven road courses before," Stewart said. "I went out to the [Bob Bondurant School of High-Performance Driving, in 1999] and had Chris Cook as my instructor there. He was really good at knowing what I needed to learn to drive a Cup car. He's run a couple of Busch [Grand National] races, so he really knew what areas I needed to focus on. Having him as an instructor gave me things to think about before we went to Sonoma and Watkins Glen, and that gave me the mind-set that I could be good on road courses."

Stewart's impressive showing was also due in part to Greg Zipadelli's ability to grasp the intricacies of road-course chassis setups. Stewart noted that Zipadelli, who grew up in Connecticut, had occasionally worked road races as a mechanic in the Busch North and Featherlite Modified series.

"Obviously, [Greg] has been with a Cup team in the past that's run road courses," Stewart said. "He's got a really good ability to adapt quickly, like I feel like I do in some cases. I'm just fortunate to have a guy like that who can adapt so quickly to different styles of racing."

As a result of his own training and Zipadelli's insight, Stewart did not consider road courses to be a weakness for either himself or the team. "Not really," he said. "Everybody is kind of in the same boat. We all only run two road-course races a year. I feel like that was one of our strong suits. We were running third and had a flat tire [in 1999] at Sonoma. We ran sixth at Watkins Glen. We had some brake problems there that kept us from running any faster than we were able to run. I feel like we've got a pretty good road-course program. I feel like that's one of our assets. It's just not something that we focus really hard on because we *do* only have two races on the schedule that are road courses.

"I think we do a pretty good job of allotting the proper amount of time to the road courses. It's not that you neglect the ovals. The road courses [award] the same amount of points that an oval does. You've got to prepare in the same way, and you've got to prepare with the same intensity. We want to win both of those races, just like we wanted to win at Dover and Michigan. It's important that you do concentrate on [road courses] and not take the attitude that they're not as important as the rest of the races because there are only two of them."

Stewart's background in go-kart racing helps him adapt to the twists and turns of road racing. His "20" car is pictured here in June 2000 at the Save Mart/ Kragen 350 at Sears Point Raceway in Sonoma, California. Tom Whitmore

When asked if the Winston Cup circuit really needed road races, Stewart flashed a smile. "I think we need *dirt* races, but I don't think that's going to happen anytime soon. It doesn't matter to me. All I care about is that, every week, I've got to go out and beat all the other guys who are out on the track when they drop the green flag on Sunday. I enjoy [road courses]. To me, it's kind of a nice change of pace. It's nice to do something different twice a year."

Stewart certainly doesn't believe his background gives him an advantage over other drivers. "There are a lot of guys in the Cup Series who came from different forms of motorsports or who have driven different divisions in the past," Stewart said. "They've all probably road-raced at some point in their careers. You look at Jerry Nadeau. He's got a good road-racing background. There are guys who drove road races before they got here, so I don't think I'm any better than anyone else.

"I came here because this was the style of racing that I really wanted to do. I felt it suited my driving style better than the other forms of racing that I was running. It's nice to know that the series you're in is going to be around 10 years from now instead of wondering year to year what's going to happen. It's hard enough to go out and do our jobs each week without having to listen to two different organizations [an obvious reference to the rival CART and IRL circuits] bicker back and forth with each other and have to listen to everybody else bicker about it. It's nice to come here and know that it has such a good fan following and that it's a stable and solid series."

Rusty Wallace captured his sixth pole of the season, but the ease with which he set a track record drew the attention of NASCAR inspectors. The Ford driver's lap, 98.711 miles per hour, was completed in nearly a half-second less than the runner-up, Kyle Petty, who ran 98.639.

In response, the ruling body took the unusual step of publicly "undressing" Wallace's car. On Saturday afternoon, less than 24 hours before the race, officials invited rival engine builders to a "tear-down" of the engine that had propelled Wallace to his record lap. Not only would NASCAR's officials discover what the Wallace engine department was doing deep within the recesses of the cylinder heads and manifold, they would also reveal the secrets to any other interested parties. Among them were car owners Jack Roush and Larry McClure, and Doug Yates, head engine builder for his father Robert's Ford teams.

Stewart, whose average speed was 98.544 mph, qualified fourth, behind only Wallace, Petty, and teammate Bobby Labonte. Jeff Gordon, who had won the circuit's five previous road-course events, qualified fifth.

In Saturday morning's practice session, the engine failed in Stewart's orange and white Pontiac, but since it was not the engine the team planned to use in Sunday's SaveMart/Kragen 350, no one seemed concerned.

Concern arrived on race morning, however. Stewart was ill. He arose late, as usual, but the effects of an intestinal flu that had begun affecting him Saturday were immediately evident. He was congested, ashen-faced, clammy, and unshaven when he arrived in the garage area. The chief question wasn't whether Stewart could win on a road course but whether he could endure nearly three hours of shifting gears, turning right and left, and slithering uphill and down in a race car not designed for such terrain.

Once the race began, it seemed as if the person who was driving the No. 20 Pontiac was different from the person speaking on the team's radio frequency. As Stewart weakly maintained that he could not possibly last the race, he nevertheless managed to keep the car in contention.

Stewart made it past the halfway mark and seemed unwilling to give up the driver's seat as long as he was able to stay near the front of the pack. On the 68th lap of the race, Stewart briefly took the lead, having slipped past both Gordon's Chevrolet and the Ford of rookie Scott Pruett. Stewart and Pruett were racing inches apart from one another until Pruett's Taurus finally tapped Stewart's Grand Prix, sending Stewart skidding off course. Seconds later, Pruett spun again, enabling Gordon, who eventually won, to take the lead.

Meanwhile, having exhausted any chance of winning, Stewart drove into the pit area and turned his car over to John Andretti. "With the accident over there, I'm not sure I could have hustled it all the way back through those cars to get back to the front," Stewart said. "The car was capable. I wasn't capable with the way I was feeling."

Andretti's own Pontiac had expired after only 15 laps, making him available and demonstrating one of the reasons that racing grudges rarely linger. It had been Andretti, just a week earlier, who had angered Stewart by racing him so aggressively in the waning laps at Pocono. Now it was Andretti whose impressive effort enabled Stewart to get a decent finish. Winston Cup points are awarded to the driver who starts a race, so when Andretti took over Stewart's car in 27th place and drove all the way back to 10th at the finish, Stewart was as grateful as he had been miffed the week before.

And Rusty Wallace? The pole winner led the first 10 laps and only one more afterward. His Ford finished on the lead lap, but in 26th place.

Gordon, setting a record by winning his sixth straight NASCAR road race, was highly complimentary of Stewart afterward. He did not know that Stewart had been ill, nor did he see any evidence of it on the track. "Scott [Pruett] was on old tires, and he was fading, but Tony was going to be tough," Gordon said. "I tell you, he was pretty strong. He made some passes on some guys in front of me that I couldn't make. You never know until you go long runs on old tires, but here, track position is so important. When [Stewart] got in front of me [on lap 66], I wasn't real happy about it. I was certainly going to try to keep the pressure on him, but when he had those problems, it definitely changed the race.

"Getting behind anyone would have been a handful, but getting behind him certainly would have been. He's a great driver and very versatile on all types of tracks. I see him coming into his own on road courses."

While Gordon was singing the praises of Stewart, Gordon's first-year crew chief, Robbie Loomis, was singing the praises of Gordon. "When I walk into every racetrack, if I can give [Gordon] the car, I know he can get the job done," Loomis said.

19

TONY'S BAND OF MERRY MEN

DAYTONA BEACH, Fla.
July 2000

Hanging around Tony Stewart's Home Depot team at Joe Gibbs Racing can be a startling experience. Insults are tossed around with brazen regularity. Irreverence flows like white water. It is best to check one's ego at the door to the transporter. Nicknames abound. Stewart is "Smoke," not because he smokes, of course, but because he is elusive: as a driver, "gone like smoke." Greg Zipadelli is "Zippy." The pit crew's gas man, Jeff Patterson, is also known as "Gooch." Why? "I don't know," Patterson says. "I guess it's because Tony calls me 'Gooch.'"

Good answer.

While stock car racing is centered in the Southeast, the team's roster reads like a list of Notre Dame recruits. They hail from all corners of the country: "Gooch" and Gordy Arbitter from California; Chris Woodward from New Hampshire and Dave Rogers from Vermont; Zipadelli, Jason Shapiro, and Jay Barry from Connecticut; Tom Dean from New Jersey; Chris Gillin from Pennsylvania; Marcus Bonicelli from Colorado; Scott Diehl and Brian Larson from Michigan; Allen Copley and Mike Lingerfelt from the Carolinas; Mark Robertson from Virginia; Jerold Shires from West Virginia; Chad Boltz from Florida;

and, finally, Ronny Crooks from the racing capital of Hueytown, Alabama, home of the legendary Allison family, the late Neil Bonnett, and Red Farmer.

All are dedicated workaholics, the cream that has risen to the top from short tracks all over the country. If not for a bit of fun now and then they would all be at each other's throats out of sheer desperation and a lethal overdose of familiarity.

One of the leading targets of insult and practical joking is Stewart, who gets as good as he gives. It is not uncommon to hear the driver taken to task: "Mister Bigshot Driver can't drive it unless it's *perfect!*" One suspects there are drivers in the Winston Cup Series with egos that could not abide such ribbing. Within the confines of the team, though, Stewart is about as regular a guy as a 29-year-old superstar can be. He enjoys the company of "the guys" infinitely more than that of visiting dignitaries or celebrities. He and Zipadelli occasionally go fishing. The team, Stewart included, has been known to go bowling together. It is said that Stewart is never more intense than when engaged in go-kart racing against members of his own team.

During the season's many rain delays, the pit crew reinvented itself as a comedy troupe. The vehicle was a fictitious radio show dubbed "Good Morning, Black Sheep."

"It is a show that talks a lot about the truth," said Jason Shapiro. "We like to talk about controversy and things that happen throughout the garage: some incident, a practice wreck, or whatever. We tell people [i.e., each other] what really happened. When a man's faster, you've got to let him go. You know what I'm saying? That's what happened, and that's we talk about."

One of the show's chief activities was a fundraiser, Shapiro said, tongue in cheek. He was the crewman who had been fined $2,000 by

NASCAR for his role in the minor scuffle between Stewart and Robby Gordon that occurred during practice before the Daytona 500.

"We had a telethon in Daytona to raise money for the producer of the show, me, since I owed NASCAR some money," Shapiro said. "There are four main guys in it. Tony Stewart and I are the original founders slash producers. Tim Carmichael was a founding member, but he's back at the shop [not working at the tracks] now. Mark Robertson has come in as an associate producer. That's pretty much the gang that does the show now. Other than that, there's not much else to do during a rain delay.

"But now that we have the show, rain delays aren't so bad."

Zipadelli holds it all together, being by far the most serious of a generally fun-loving, free-wheeling fraternity.

Of course, during the dark days of May, the team was often rife with tension. As the season went on, the team matured by learning how to act, on occasion, immature. Stewart and his partners in crime became rather adept at responding to the sport's omnipresent rumor mill by feeding it. Their schemes were typically born as several crewmen lounged in either the front of the team's transporter or Stewart's motor-coach, watching the Saturday Busch Grand National race.

At one point, a rumor made the rounds that Jimmy Makar, Bobby Labonte's crew chief, was going to be elevated to overall manager of Joe Gibbs Racing. Zipadelli, supposedly, was to be moved over to Labonte's team as crew chief, with Gibbs hiring someone else to direct Stewart's operation.

"In all the meetings we've had, that has never been mentioned one time," Stewart said, conspiratorially. "We just figured out that we would see how far it would go if we just didn't do anything to discourage it. When I get asked about it, I just say, you know, 'Could be. If it's been in the newspaper, I guess there must be something to it.' We didn't actually say yes, but we didn't say no.'

"The next thing I think we're going to plant is that Joe [Gibbs] reached the top of pro football, and now he's done well in NASCAR, so he's looking for new worlds to conquer. We're trying to figure out how we can spread the rumor that Joe is going to start his own Indy-car team, that he wants to win the Indianapolis 500, or the CART championship, or maybe Formula One. There's really no limit to how outrageous you can be."

By developing a certain sense of the absurd, the team managed to ease some of the tension of a grueling season.

20

ANGST ON THE BANKS

DAYTONA BEACH, Florida
July 2000

Tony Stewart had little reason to celebrate his return to Daytona International Speedway for the Pepsi 400, third of four "restrictor-plate" races in the Winston Cup Series. He approached the race with teeth gritted, trying to be as upbeat as possible despite his dislike for the horsepower limitations and the resulting strategy changes, which he found bewildering.

Two years earlier, lights had been installed at the 2.5-mile, high-banked track, thus enabling the summertime race to be contested at night. The first nighttime running, in 1998, had been postponed until October because of devastating wildfires that swept through northern Florida. The following year, Dale Jarrett's victory had been somewhat unsatisfying because the race ended under caution. The race was nevertheless a commercial success, sold out for the first time in memory.

This time around, the pre-race publicity had apparently been hindered by tepid public response to the Daytona 500. The problem was a lack of passing. Jarrett, who had not won in the 15 races since, dominated a race that elicited the fewest lead changes, nine, of any 500 in 35 years. In the weeks leading up to the summertime race, telemarketers had been employed to boost sagging ticket sales. Still the race did not sell out, and International Speedway Corporation would cite declining ticket revenues in a disappointing earnings report released later in the year.

The previous restrictor-plate race, at Talladega on April 16, had been the site of the 11-car accident that involved both Stewart and teammate Bobby Labonte. At the time, the two drivers had been working together in the aerodynamic draft, trying to get their cars up near the front in time to play some role in the race's outcome.

Because of the difficulty in moving up through the pack with restrictor plates sapping the engines of so much horsepower—an estimated 40 percent—Stewart and Labonte knew they could ill afford another poor qualifying performance. What had put them in position to become entangled in the Talladega crash was the fact that neither started in the top 35 positions of the 43-car grid.

"We'll have to see where we start," Stewart said. "We planned our race strategy off where we started. A lot can happen. We'll just have to see how we qualify, but we obviously want to stay up at the front for the majority of the night race. If we qualify badly, then we'll need to take care of our equipment. It's a lot harder to run wide open at night in the middle of the summer here. You've really got to work on the handling of your car. That's really important, but we'll just see how the circumstances play out and go from there."

NASCAR had granted the Pontiacs the tiniest of rule concessions in the period between Talladega and Daytona. The rear bumpers had been slightly reshaped, but neither Stewart nor Labonte had been able to notice a change in performance during races on shorter tracks.

"I think at a track the size of Daytona, we'll be able to notice the difference," Stewart said optimistically, "but it's so hot at Daytona that you're kind of comparing apples to oranges. Even though we're returning to Daytona, it's so hot, and the track temperatures are so much higher [than in February for the Daytona 500] that it's a different racetrack. Even though we're racing at night, the car ends up driving differently because the track gets so slippery."

The only adjustment Stewart intended to make was to change the visor on his helmet to shield some of the glare of the lights. "Other than that, I don't know what we're going to change, to be honest. Last year, that race was so different from what the 500 was. I enjoyed it. I thought it was a fun race because you could only run about four laps wide open, and the rest of the time, you were searching around on the racetrack for an area where your car drove well. It made it more of a challenge," he said.

Stewart had finished a respectable sixth at Daytona the previous summer, and that race had been run more than two months before Stewart's first win, September 11, 1999, at Richmond.

Stewart said a driver's perception of speed is pretty much the same, whether you're racing in daylight or under the glare of the specially designed lighting system. "It looks a lot faster from the grandstands, I know that," he said. "It's just a lot of fun. I like racing at night. Being able to run a track this size at night is a pretty neat feeling."

Stewart, a late riser who typically had to be roused by aide Judy Dominick in order to make pre-race driver's meetings for most Sunday races, had found that night racing made him feel more energetic and rested. "I'm nocturnal, basically," Stewart said. "The best hours of the day for me begin when the sun goes down. I'm a lot sharper and a lot wider awake at night."

Stewart needed every bit of that sharpness for the high-speed chess game of drafting. He made no secret that he was uncomfortable having to rely on other drivers to help him pass, a necessary evil in restrictor-plate racing. Stewart was not alone in his dislike for what racing at Daytona had become. Dale Earnhardt, who had won more total races (i.e., including divisions besides just Winston Cup) than any other driver in the track's history, was even more vocal than Stewart.

"I wish we could just race," growled Earnhardt. "We go to Pocono, Loudon, and these places and race and have a good time. We come here, and it's aggravation just to get through inspection, just to get through inspection for qualifying.

"You qualify, and it's more aggravation getting out of that mess and changing your cars over to race. Dang, let's race. If they'll take the restrictor plates off, they won't have to worry about springs and shocks and stuff. People will have those damn blades [spoilers] up in the air hollering, 'I need more spoiler [to slow down].'

"I think all the drivers and teams are frustrated with the way they have to race here. Have you heard a postive comment from anyone? I wish there was something we could do. I wish there was something NASCAR could do. I'm not condemning anybody. I wish there was another solution [besides restrictor plates]. I don't think anyone is happy doing what we're doing. It's more of a chess game. If you end up in the right place and make the right move, then you're going to be a hero. If you don't, you're going to be a zero."

Stewart lacked Earnhardt's knack for drafting, but he was trying to grasp the nuances of positioning—whether to be in the outside line, inside line, or sometimes even the middle line—that allow a driver to successfully execute passes. Mostly what he had learned was not to try to pass, and to move up when others tried and failed. That tack might produce a decent finish, but not a victory, since a race leader would have no need to pass.

"Whoever you're around is your drafting partner," said Stewart.

"Last year, I thought I was going to run with a certain group of guys, but I ended up lapping about half of them. You never know. You've just got to take what it [the draft] gives you. The important thing is that you have to have people to draft with. I don't think it's a situation where you pick out who you're going to be with; it's just whoever is around you at the time."

Greg Zipadelli suggested that the only solution to the problem was to reduce the slope of Daytona's 31-degree banking in the turns. "It seems that NASCAR has tried really hard at doing some things," Zipadelli said. "The thing I would suggest, but they probably wouldn't like it, is knocking the banks down and building a two-and-a-half-mile flat track. I mean, we run so well at flat tracks . . . Why not?

"Seriously, I don't know that there is an answer. They tried some things with the Craftsman Trucks [an auxiliary series that had debuted at Daytona in February] that looked like they might work out pretty well, but, as we all saw, there was an awful lot of damage [crashes] that came from that race. I don't know if there's an answer to it. They [NASCAR] keep working on it [to slow the cars down], and we keep making our cars better, faster . . . I sure would like to see something change."

During time trials, the same drivers who were fastest in the first visit to Daytona, Jarrett and teammate Ricky Rudd, swept the front row again. Jarrett averaged 187.547 miles per hour, besting Rudd by just over a tenth of a second and just under half a mile per hour. Fords captured the first three positions—veteran Bill Elliott was third—but Pontiacs were fourth, sixth, and seventh, Stewart occupying the last of those spots. Jerry Nadeau qualified eighth in the field's fastest Chevrolet. Labonte qualified 21st in the other Joe Gibbs Pontiac.

The conservative NASCAR braintrust's choice for president,

George W. Bush, was the race's Grand Marshal, though CBS was understandably reluctant to give the Texas governor a free commercial on Saturday-night prime time. The free commercial was limited to the nearly 170,000 fans in attendance, but the speedway's president, ex-banker John Graham, gave the GOP nominee a worshipful send-off. Among Bush's comments was the rather self-serving observation that all the drivers were personal friends of his family.

Amidst presidential politics and enough fireworks to inspire a national anthem, the actual race turned out to be another dud. The winner of the Pepsi 400 did not sweep into the lead by means of some gaudy move on the high banks. He did it by changing two tires instead of four. Credit the winning decision to Jeff Burton's crew chief, Frankie Stoddard.

"I followed the guy in the lead all night long," noted Burton with surprising candor, "and it was real hard to pass him, so Frank wanted the lead [prompting the more economical choice of tires]."

Stewart somehow managed to slipstream his way up from seventh at the start to second in the first few laps, which was about the most exciting occurrence of the night. He led a single lap, the 54th, but was in the top three for probably a majority of the 160. At the end, Stewart had to settle for sixth, exactly the same finish as in the previous year's race, largely because he opted for four new tires instead of two in the final pit stop.

"Two tires got us our track position, got us in front of the crowd, and it was very difficult to pass," observed Burton. "Passing was hard, and I was fast enough to block and stay in the way enough to be a pain.

"I just decided, if [runner-up] Jarrett was going to get by me, he was going to have to knock me out of the way. I knew, if he got alongside me, I'd have finished 15th."

For the second time in 2000, it seemed a shame that racing at Daytona, NASCAR's flagship track, had come to this.

Stewart mostly muttered afterward, his carefully contrived optimism gone by the wayside. At one point he pounded his fist against a counter and growled fiercely, "I hate it. This ain't racing."

21

TRAGEDY CLOSE TO HOME

LOUDON, New Hampshire
July 2000

Tony Stewart was still in the transporter, putting on his uniform for the first practice session on Friday morning. He was running a bit late, but practice was just getting started, and only a few cars were on the track. That's why the impact could be heard so clearly. Boom! It was a loud, sickening noise that immediately caught the attention of everyone milling about in the New Hampshire International Speedway garage.

The Chevrolet Monte Carlo driven by Kenny Irwin Jr. had just hit the third-turn wall, the same wall that had claimed the life of Adam Petty on May 12.

Within seconds, a crowd had gathered at the edge of the garage nearest the accident. When emergency workers removed Irwin from his crumpled car, he appeared limp, but from a distance, it was unclear whether he was unconscious or perhaps just woozy. But the blood was visible as he was placed on a stretcher, and as the ambulance drove away, the crowd immediately migrated to the infield hospital, a small building located near turn four, just 25 yards or so from the media center.

Nothing about the behavior of the officials at the care center dissuaded observers from the belief that this was a serious accident. The emergency vehicles were positioned to block the view of bystanders as Irwin was transferred from the ambulance. Veteran observers sensed a fatal or near-fatal accident from the unmistakable signs: the wreckage being quickly covered and carted away from the property, reporters and photographers being shooed and shoved out of the area, all emergency activity concealed or blocked from public view.

The crash occurred at 11:23 a.m., on Friday, July 7, within yards of the site of Petty's death. Irwin's Chevrolet had skidded out of control, by all accounts the result of a stuck throttle, and smashed into the solid concrete wall separating the track from the grandstands. The car had spewed tire smoke as Irwin frantically applied his brakes. It rode up the wall sideways and flipped over on its roof, coming to a rest between turns three and four.

Apparently, Irwin died soon after the accident. NASCAR officials waited for some time before confirming the 30-year-old driver's death, and then the brief report, citing "multiple injuries," came ostensibly from the hospital in nearby Concord. In the hour after the crash, only a few people, among them Irwin's crew chief, Tony Glover, and Miss Winston, Renee Perks, were allowed entry into the care center. No medical helicopter was ever requested: Irwin had been transported by ambulance to the hospital where he was declared dead.

Irwin was the first Winston Cup driver to die from an on-track incident since Neil Bonnett and Rodney Orr died within days of each other at Daytona in 1994. (Adam Petty had been competing in the Busch Grand National division.) Those deaths also occurred in practice sessions.

NASCAR carried on with qualifying on the day of the former Rookie of the Year's death. Mike Helton, NASCAR's chief operating officer, was not at the track when the fatal crash occurred, but he would later say, "As much as our hearts may not be into it, we press on to deliver our product and make sure the communities here are in place and intact when we come back.

"It's difficult, and everybody deals with it in his own form and fashion, but we have a very big responsibility, and it's hard, sometimes, to go on with it, but we feel like it is necessary to. It's not just a show. NASCAR is more like a community, and if the citizen of a community passes away, the community still has to go on, the lights still have to work, the water has to run, life has to go on. . . . Your heart may not be in it 100 percent necessarily, but it has to go on. That's the way we look at our schedules.

"It could have been that we didn't press on [Friday], but I don't know if that would've made it any better. I think a lot of people, for the most part, would [rather] stay busy, but our procedures are to press on in cases like this. It's not that we don't have a heart or soul. It's simply because we have a lot of responsibilities—everybody does in the garage area—to a lot of different people. The biggest thing is that's what we do: we race. That's what Kenny did: he raced. That's what Adam [Petty] did: he raced."

It would be inaccurate to describe Tony Stewart and Kenny Irwin as friends. They had been rivals, bitter rivals, for almost a decade. They both grew up in Indiana, their paths to stardom almost mirroring one another.

In a very real sense, Stewart knew Irwin better than one knows a friend. He had observed Irwin with a competitor's eye, identifying his strengths and weaknesses. Now Irwin was dead, and the guilt from all the strife between the two flooded into Stewart's consciousness. He went about his business quietly. He qualified sixth for the laughably titled Thatlook.com 300. He immediately dispatched pilot Bob Burris to Indianapolis, where his plane was to be used to cater to any need of the Irwin family.

After hearing of Irwin's death, Stewart had reflected on their many battles on the open-wheel ovals of the Midwest, where both had compiled stellar records and won championships. He recalled a dirt race in which the two had been teammates and had fought so fiercely that they both crashed, raising the dander of the man who had built their cars, Bob East. Stewart knew that the rivalry had prevented him from having conversations with Irwin he might otherwise have had. With Irwin dead, Stewart realized there were dozens of things he wanted to say to him. "I don't understand why things like this happen to guys like him who have paid their dues and worked really hard to get to this level," Stewart said. "It just doesn't seem fair. The thing I keep thinking about is how bad his family hurts right now, because his family has been behind him ever since I met him in 1991. I know how important racing was in their lives, and how close a family they were . . . so I'm thinking about them right now."

Stewart's most famous incident in the Winston Cup Series had been the exchange of sheet metal, gestures, and invective with Irwin at Martinsville the previous October. "We always had a love-hate relationship," Stewart said. "Ever since I met Kenny, when we were running for the rookie-of-the-year title at the Indianapolis Speedrome, we both raced each other hard. From then on, it's been a rivalry that continued right up to now.

"Through nine years of rivalry, though, there's been a mutual admiration, a respect, for each other and for what each could do in a race car. Of all the years I've raced, I think I can honestly say, sitting up here and thinking about it all day, of all the people I've ever raced with, Kenny was the hardest and toughest racer I've ever had to race on a daily or weekly basis.

Stewart (left), pictured here with Greg Zipa- delli, racked up another win at New Hampshire International Speedway in July 2000. The vic- tory was bittersweet, however, due to the tragic death of rival Kenny Irwin Jr. during a pre-race practice ses- sion. Tom Whitmore

"It didn't matter whether it was a sprint car on pavement on Friday night or a midget on dirt on Saturday night, or a Silver Crown car on dirt on Sunday. You knew that you had to be on your game because, if you weren't, he was going to beat you. I've said this a thousand times since I started in Winston Cup: Kenny's part of the reason I got here, because he pushed me to make myself better each week. There are not a lot of guys who worked any harder than Kenny to get where he got in his racing career."

The week of Irwin's death, Stewart had a bit of a scare himself. One of his prop plane's two engines had lost power forcing an emergency landing at an airport in Asheville, North Carolina, on Wednesday night, July 5. Burris had dealt with the problem expertly and landed the plane without incident.

"It was really no big deal, to be honest with you," Stewart had said upon arriving in New Hampshire. "It sounds a lot more dramatic than it really was. Asheville just wasn't really in our plans, so I guess they have to call that an emergency landing. Bob [Burris] just did what he knew he had to do when he got the instrument readings he was getting. . . . I didn't think there was anything to worry about until I saw fire engines pulling up on the runway.

"Don't get me wrong—I really do appreciate all the fans who have been concerned about it—but there is nothing to be worried about. Believe it or not, I'm actually more confident now in the safety of air travel than I was before."

Naturally, given the mood of the weekend, race day in New England arrived dark and foreboding. Stewart went out and won the race, which was shortened from 300 to 273 laps after two rain delays. Stewart dominated the event, leading 156 laps, but it took a bit of luck to nail it down. Had the race not been shortened, Stewart and runner-up Joe Nemechek would have had to pit for fuel near the end, and third-place finisher Mark Martin, who made his previous stop later than Stewart and Nemechek, would have been able to go the distance.

"Thank goodness [Greg Zipadelli] never told me to try to save fuel because I don't know how to save fuel, anyway," said Stewart, who had lost the same race a year earlier when he ran out of gas with two laps to go. "To shut the motor off is the only way I know to save fuel. He told me after the [first] red flag, 'Go hard. Go hard and try to get as many guys down as you can.' That way, when we did have to come in, we could build up as much time [on his pursuers] as we could."

Stewart, who had lost the Las Vegas race due to rain, had now won twice in races that ended prematurely. He said he felt Irwin's presence in the car late in the race. He had experienced the same eerie feeling in 1996, at Indianapolis, after another teammate, Scott Brayton, had been killed before the 500.

Ruefully, Stewart said that he had spoken to Irwin's ghostly presence: "Hey, big buddy, a bucket of water right now wouldn't hurt us any.'

"He made me wait a little longer than I wanted to wait for it, though," Stewart added. "I don't know if he brought the rain or not. He is probably busy at the check-in counter up there or something. He probably made me sweat for it a little bit.

"That's like him," Stewart said, and he smiled and looked past his audience of reporters, focusing on some distant point through moistened eyes.

22

A NEW BALANCE

LONG POND, Pennsylvania
July 2000

A week off followed New Hampshire, giving Tony Stewart more time to ponder the death of Kenny Irwin. He arrived at the next race, the Pennsylvania 500, still affected by the loss.

"I probably spent more time with the Irwins than I had in the previous nine years," Stewart said.

An old legend holds that stock car racers, in particular, avoid funerals because they remind them of their own mortality. They all know the danger is there, but they don't want to confront it any more than necessary. Stewart, however, didn't hesitate to attend Kenny Irwin's funeral.

"He worked really hard to get to this level," Stewart said. "He was always a hands-on guy. He could probably have built a Winston Cup car from scratch if he had to; I couldn't.

"That shows how dedicated he was to auto racing. He always was working on his own race cars and making decisions on what to change. He was probably one of the most focused guys at the racetrack. We can't bring him back. There is nothing we can do. I guarantee you I'd do anything I could to bring him back right now. It was a lot of fun racing with him. It was frustrating at times, but that's just because we were so competitive with each other. But I'd rather have him here, and I'd do anything I could to get him back right now."

With three victories under his belt and a week off to contemplate the season, Stewart took the time to analyze his performance. His rookie season, by comparison, had seemed effortless, perhaps because now so much more was expected of him. Stewart had become a familiar face, an established star, and the public scrutiny seemed to weigh heavily on him. Still, he was tired of talking about the off-track adjustments he'd had to make. When the second Pocono Raceway event beckoned, Stewart instead preferred talking about what he had learned about driving stock cars in general and his car in particular.

"I think I've learned a lot that held me back at the beginning of last year," Stewart said. "We had a lot better team than we had a race-car driver for the first half of [1999]. I started catching up a little bit as the year went on. This year, I feel like I'm gaining more knowledge. I've worked with the same guys. We haven't switched any of our guys over [to Joe Gibbs' other team], so the guys that I'm working with, I'm more familiar with them, and they're more familiar with me.

"I'm just starting to get smarter. Every time we make a change, Greg [Zipadelli] lets me know why we're changing it, what it's supposed to do. I'm starting to get more involved with that, so it makes me more confident as a driver, knowing what the changes are. Knowing how the car should react every time I go on the track is just making me a more confident race-car driver."

Perhaps another reason Stewart seemed calmer was that he and Krista Dwyer, to whom he had been engaged, were back together. It had taken some time to get past the frosty silence that followed the breakup, and this time there were no commitments, no plans to marry. Basically, the two had just decided to give it another try and see how it worked out.

Stewart won his first pole of the season at Pocono Raceway in July 2000. His average speed of 172.391 miles per hour established a track record. Tom Whitmore

A reporter asked Stewart about the demands on his private life, a point of contention earlier in the year, but Stewart deflected the question by observing how much more difficult the situation was for other drivers who had more commitments than he did.

"I don't think one guy can answer that," he said. "You're asking a guy like me who doesn't have a wife and family to support. I don't have plays and softball and baseball games to go watch my kids play, whereas some of these other drivers do. I don't want to speak for them, but I'm sure it's harder on them to a certain degree."

It was common knowledge that NASCAR intended to increase by

two the number of races in 2001, adding events in the Chicago and Kansas City areas at newly constructed facilities. As it was, there were only five open weekends between early February and late November.

"It [the new schedule] takes two weekends where they would be able to spend with their families," Stewart said. "It takes that away from them, so I'm sure it's going to be a little harder on them. But it doesn't matter to me. All it means to me is that I have to cut two or three dirt-track races out of my schedule, so it doesn't affect me too much."

When Stewart arrived at Pocono Raceway for the season's second visit, he seemed notably more relaxed. Whether it was the sobering effect of Irwin's death and funeral, or the reunion with his girlfriend, not even Stewart could say.

Stewart's calmness had no effect on his driving, though. He won the pole for the first time all season, and his average speed, 172.391 mph, established a track record. His time, 52.207 seconds, was .233 seconds faster than Rusty Wallace's speed just five weeks earlier.

"Every week, you've got to treat it as two events," Stewart cautioned. "Qualifying is one event, and the race is another. It's two totally different packages under the hood [NASCAR teams commonly use separate engines for time trials and races]. Now we have to worry about the other half of the event and try to get the car right [for the race] like we did for qualifying."

Stewart's caution proved well-founded. Joe Gibbs had the pole sitter in Stewart and the winner of both 1999 Pocono races in Bobby Labonte, but as it turned out, another owner, Roger Penske, had the two drivers who would settle the Pennsylvania 500: Rusty Wallace and Jeremy Mayfield.

Wallace sped past Mayfield on the final lap. Mayfield, who had won the earlier race at the 2.5-mile track by bumping Dale Earnhardt's Chevrolet in the final turn, had a flat tire this time. Earnhardt might have taken a certain satisfaction in Mayfield's misfortune had he not finished 25th.

Stewart never led a lap, not even the first, when Wallace swept by after starting on the outside of the front row. He went on to win by .126 of a second over Jeff Burton as Mayfield's disabled Taurus limped home 10th. The Fords, in fact, took four of the first five positions, joined only by Jeff Gordon's Chevrolet in third. The only solace for Gibbs was that Labonte finished sixth in the highest-finishing Pontiac.

Mayfield, by the way, was not the only driver to suffer tire problems. A cut tire cost Stewart a lap, and he finished 26th, one spot behind Earnhardt.

23

ZIPPY

INDIANAPOLIS, Indiana
August 2000

The man who directs Tony Stewart's team is methodical and, at least by the standards of those around him, rather quiet. Greg Zipadelli has a certain economy to his words and actions. It is not unusual to find Zipadelli in the lounge of the team transporter, painstakingly making notes while Stewart watches satellite TV on the couch. Stewart is rarely unaccompanied, but Zipadelli seems oblivious to the parade of visitors. He is capable of blocking out the world while meticulously working at the task at hand.

"There are a lot of people out here making a living in racing," Zipadelli said, "but there is only a small group of guys doing it with the passion of Saturday-night short-track racers."

Zipadelli understands that passion. He grew up in a racing family. As a youngster, he worked with his Uncle Billy on a modified owned by his father, Charles, in his native Connecticut. Now 33, Zipadelli has made a full-time career of racing, breaking into the business a decade ago when he accepted a job as Mike McLaughlin's crew chief in the NASCAR Featherlite Modified Tour. Later, Zipadelli joined Mike Stefanik on the Busch North Series, where Stefanik won a championship in 1997. The following year, Zipadelli moved south to become a chassis specialist at Roush Racing, where he worked under Frankie Stoddard with driver Jeff Burton.

Joe Gibbs still marvels at how Zipadelli, a rookie crew chief in Winston Cup, managed to find success so quickly while working with a rookie driver, Stewart, in 1999.

"I thought it was crazy," Gibbs said. "The last thing I wanted to do was put Tony with a guy who had never headed up a Winston Cup team. I wanted an experienced guy, but Jimmy [Makar, Bobby Labonte's crew chief] and I sat down, and Jimmy said, 'The more I look at it, I think [Zipadelli] is the guy.' I really could never have visualized doing what we did, but I also believe in trusting your instincts, and if Jimmy thought this was the guy, I decided to go with what he thought.

"What they've done together amazes me every day."

During the erratic beginning of Stewart's second season, Zipadelli was a perpetual voice of reason. "Tony and I have hit it off well," said Zipadelli, occasionally prone to understatement. "We're close in age, both kind of aggressive. We've been even more successful than we thought we'd be at this point."

Zipadelli *is* aggressive, making the hard behind-the-scenes decisions and trusting his instincts, but unlike Stewart, he tends to keep his emotions in check.

"My core group knows the car front to back, and we can sit down and talk about almost anything," Zipadelli said. "I think some teams are a little too specialized, and that can come back to bite you if you have to wait on one person to get something done."

Dealing with Stewart's hot temper is a challenge for Zipadelli, but by now, he has developed an instinctive knack. In their radio communications during races, Stewart's emotions sometimes flare.

Rather than get emotional himself, Zipadelli patiently points out key facts—how many laps to go, when to pit, lap times, separations between cars—and gently encourages Stewart.

"This sport is emotional," Zipadelli said. "You put in a lot of time and emotion. It's hard to control your emotions. On the positive side, that's what makes Tony Stewart such a passionate person. People don't want to look past what he just said. Well, he's a winner. He's not a good loser. That's what makes him special. He's not a lot of fun in tough moments, but that fierce competitiveness is what this sport is all about."

In the heat of battle, both Zipadelli and Stewart direct their intensity to the task at hand: Stewart applies his rush of adrenaline to winning races, and Zipadelli oversees everything in the pits and makes sure nothing goes amiss. Afterwards, when the atmosphere is less frenetic, both are prone to being impatient and perhaps even a tad petulant.

Once Zipadelli, busily loading up a battered car after a disappointing race, was asked by a reporter to confirm a story the reporter had heard elsewhere in the garage. The story involved a verbal exchange between Stewart and another driver, and it was more amusing than controversial.

"You don't have to write a thing about that," Zipadelli said, quickly considering it better to err on the side of caution. "I can't tell you what to write, but you don't *have* to write it."

"Well, sure I do," the reporter replied. "It's my job. It's not being critical . . . it's being funny."

"You can write anything you want," Zipadelli snapped, and then he disappeared into the transporter, having, in effect, just confirmed the story by the way he reacted to it.

On occasion, the crew chief and driver get away from the pressure and competition by fishing together. They have been known to retire to a local pond after a long day at the track. They enjoy the shared solitude, and perhaps there they bare their souls. It is unlikely, however, that the conversation strays far from racing. Neither seems to have much interest in anything else.

24

NO PLACE LIKE INDY

INDIANAPOLIS, Indiana
August 2000

The choice of "home tracks" attests to the nomadic lifestyle of NASCAR drivers. Jeff Gordon claims Indianapolis Motor Speedway as his home track because he moved to nearby Pittsboro, Indiana, when he was a teenager. He also claims Sears Point because he was born in nearby Vallejo, California, and Dover because Delaware is the base of operations for his sponsor, DuPont. Rusty Wallace claims Bristol because he owns several automobile dealerships in eastern Tennessee, and beginning in 2001, he will surely claim the Kansas City track, because he grew up in Missouri. (Never mind that the track is actually located in Kansas.) Almost every driver claims Lowe's Motor Speedway because most NASCAR teams are headquartered near Charlotte.

No such waffling exists in Tony Stewart's mind. Gordon moved to Indiana because the state would allow him to race sprint cars before he could drive on its highways. Stewart is all Hoosier, born and raised, through and through. He grows misty-eyed at the singing of "Back Home Again in Indiana." He no longer races in the Indianapolis 500, but he has not given up dreams of one day winning it. The Brickyard

400, NASCAR's annual visit to Indianapolis Motor Speedway, is the highlight of Stewart's year.

"It [the Brickyard 400] is not going to replace winning the Indy 500 by any means," Stewart said, "but you always want to win at home. I want to win every race I run, anyway, but would I trade the Loudon [New Hampshire] win in for this? Yeah. I'd do it in a heartbeat. I definitely want to win here pretty badly."

The old Texan A.J. Foyt, the first man to win the Indianapolis 500 four times and an adopted Hoosier, now owns a NASCAR team. Does he think the stock-car event has actually surpassed the 500 in prestige?

"Well, it's possible," Foyt conceded. "Things have changed. Of course, you've got tradition with the Indy 500, and [the Brickyard 400] would never override the tradition. I keep falling back on the Kentucky Derby. There are a lot of beautiful racetracks in horse racing, but there is only one Kentucky Derby, and there will always just be one Indy 500."

At the Brickyard, you could find Stewart by looking for the cloud of dust. He was fawned over, chased and idolized. The racers all knew him, and the rest of the population wanted to. Stewart seemed to be everywhere during the week: at Indianapolis Raceway Park in Clermont to race USAC Silver Crown cars, at autograph sessions and personal appearances, and at the annual Tony Stewart Fan Club picnic, scheduled for the day after the race.

Not since the Daytona 500 had a NASCAR event been so full of news. Balloons were raised in Kenny Irwin's memory on race morning. Johnny Benson announced a sponsor for the remainder of the year. Chip Ganassi, a highly successful CART owner, announced that he was buying majority interest in the two-car team of Felix Sabates. Terry Labonte's record streak of competing in 655 races came to an end when Labonte, hobbled by the broken bone in his leg and suffering from dizzy spells, reluctantly concluded he could no longer persevere. Jeremy Mayfield suffered head injuries in a Friday practice crash, and he, too, did not compete in the Brickyard 400.

A rule change required two new on-board mechanisms to prevent the dreaded "stuck throttles" that were blamed for the deaths of Irwin and Adam Petty. Hut Stricklin settled into the driving seat of the underfunded Junie Donlavey team. The two principal auxiliary series, Busch Grand National and Craftsman Truck, held races on Thursday and Friday nights at Raceway Park. Several reporters were at the "big track" dawn to dusk, then fought bumper-to-bumper traffic out to Clermont to cover the night races Stewart's Silver Crown race, which had been scheduled for Wednesday night, fell victim to a thunderstorm of almost biblical proportions. Undaunted, Stewart went back out there after his Sunday picnic—the Brickyard 400 was run on Saturday—and finished second.

Stewart was a veritable perpetual-motion machine, and no one else was getting much rest, either. The circus-like atmosphere invigorated Stewart, though, in ways that no other place, no other track, could. "Indy means as much to me as Daytona means to everybody else," he said.

The year before, a familiar reporter had followed Stewart into his garage bay, only to find out that he'd been accompanied by a startling rush of humanity, none carrying press passes. Stewart had whirled around, a look of shock in his eyes, and blurted, "Get these people the hell out of here!"

Security guards had dutifully complied, shooing the mass back out into the lane between the garage buildings. The reporter had exited with them. Stewart then pursued the reporter.

"Not you," he said.

Sheepishly, the reporter muttered, "Well, Tony, you've got every right to tell me when I'm out of line," whereupon Stewart consented to the brief interview the reporter had sought.

That little scene occurred before Stewart had so much as won his first Winston Cup race.

Naturally, as fate would dictate, the 2000 race proved to be an anticlimax for Stewart. He finished fifth, a result altogether insufficient given the importance he placed on the event.

"About the last 20 or 25 laps, I was pretty much locked into my spot," Stewart lamented. "As long as I didn't kill the race car and kill the tires, I was pretty much going to finish where I was at. I couldn't gain on anybody in front of me, and I wasn't going to lose anything to anybody behind me. I basically just stayed in there, and at that point, I was just asking for updates as to where Bobby was."

Teammate Bobby Labonte won the race, passing Rusty Wallace on the 146th of 160 laps. The pass ended a tension-filled pursuit during which Labonte's Pontiac had shadowed Wallace's Ford lap after lap. Once clear, Labonte pulled swiftly away. After making the pass in the third turn, he and Wallace bumped at the head of the front straight, exiting turn four. By the next time around, however, Labonte was perhaps 50 yards ahead, and his margin at the end, 4.229 seconds, was the widest in the race's seven-year history.

Judged by the standards of most NASCAR events, the race had been somewhat mundane. In terms of dramatic developments, though, the week was a rousing success. The track record, 181.068 miles per hour, had been set by a driver, Brett Bodine, who qualified on the second day and thus had to start 26th. Darrell Waltrip, struggling miserably in the final year of an epochal career, had started second and then gone on to finish a respectable 11th, which ended up being nine positions better than any other performance during his entire season.

Poor Stewart. From the time he arrived for practice, his Pontiac had been a bit off. Teammate Labonte qualified third, while Stewart had to settle for 18th. "We weren't as fast as they were," Stewart said, referring to all of the other drivers who finished in front of him. "That's all there was to it. We just weren't as fast at they were. That's why you don't gain time.

"I feel real sympathetic for Michael Andretti [who has never won the Indianapolis 500] right now. It's just hard. This is a hard place to win, and that's why it's so special. When you do win here, you feel like you conquered the world, and that's because this place is so tough. I don't think you'd appreciate it if it was an easy place to win at."

When you *do* win here. When Stewart left Indianapolis, he still had a victory in his future plans.

25

SOMETIMES THE FIRE BURNS

WATKINS GLEN, New York
August 2000

As the summer wore on, Tony Stewart seemed to be learning some lessons from his early-season adversity. He had become weary of having his candor come back to haunt him, so he chose his words more carefully. At the same time, though, his fierce, competitive spirit could not be quelled, and sometimes the fire that exemplified his winning spirit still seemed at odds with the restraint required by his new celebrity.

At Watkins Glen, Jeff Burton's Ford was parked next to Stewart's Pontiac in the garage. The configuration of the building caused teams to point their cars in V-shaped order, thus affording a bit more work space. Burton's and Stewart's cars had their noses slanted inward toward each other.

A female fan circulated through the garage area, brazenly interrupting one driver after another, shoving her souvenir items in their faces and demanding autographs. Burton, a canny Virginian with a keen sense of humor, watched with amusement as she slowly worked her way toward Stewart, who was oblivious, as usual, preoccupied with discussions involving the preparation of his car.

"Watch this," Burton whispered to a reporter. "Stewart's gonna put on a show."

He and the reporter were joined by a couple of mechanics from Burton's team, all relishing the possibility of a typical Stewart explosion.

Stewart's eyes flashed with anger as the intruder forced herself upon him, but only for a split second. Stewart then quickly signed her postcard without saying a word.

"Damn!" said Burton to his little band of spies. "That's the new Tony Stewart right there." He paused, a grin breaking out. "I liked the old Tony Stewart a lot better."

So Stewart was making progress, but only grudgingly. He was chomping at the bit, torn between discretion and the strong inclination to be his old, unfettered self. For every five times Stewart would hold his tongue, gather his wits, and use his judgment, there would be one moment or incident when he just could not contain himself.

At Watkins Glen, Stewart was due for a good, old-fashioned blowup. For those who might have anticipated this moment, he did not disappoint.

The Cup series features only two road courses, so opportunities for road-race victories are rare. Stewart hadn't won any of the three road races in which he competed, but still he'd managed to make a name for himself on such courses.

"The difference between Watkins Glen and Sears Point, and the reason Watkins Glen is a more technical racetrack [to drive] is because the corners are a lot faster," Stewart observed. "If you break your momentum just a little bit, it shows up big time. Right now, we're in a string of tracks where momentum is a big factor. It seems like forward bite [traction coming out of turns] is more of an issue at Sears Point because you've got to work so hard to get the car to turn. At Watkins

Glen, you try to do as much as you can to try to keep your momentum up and not break it in any way."

Jerry Nadeau, a Stewart chum, began his career in road racing and once spent a season in Europe. "I don't mind being thought of as a road-course expert," Nadeau said, "but there are a lot of other guys like Jeff [Gordon], Rusty [Wallace], and Tony [Stewart] who are really good, too."

While Stewart was publicly humble about his chances of winning, privately, he had high hopes. It galled him when rain washed out qualifying because, based on his practice speeds, he thought he had a legitimate shot at the pole.

"During my banzai run on stickers [new tires], I was considerably faster the first half of the lap, and I got stuck in traffic, and I just aborted the run," he said. "There wasn't any use in finishing it. I knew that we could run, though. I felt confident. We had a front-row car, for sure. There's no doubt in my mind I would have sat on the front row [qualified first or second], and I'm confident I probably could have sat on the pole. I would have liked to have seen qualifying held, but at the same time, I'm comfortable with the guys starting around. If I was 40th in points, it would be a whole different story. I'm happy, at least, with the opportunity to start up front in the first three rows."

Stewart's summer of good fortune had elevated him to sixth in the season standings, and in the absence of qualifying, that was where he started. Gordon, who had won the previous six road races, began the race directly behind Stewart in eighth.

If Stewart has a driving flaw that regularly reveals itself—and it is a minor one—it is his unwillingness to be crowded, shoved, or bullied— even when it would be strategically wise. When a race is on the line, his indomitable spirit and his determination to protect his turf pay dividends, but there are times, in the early laps of a race, when it's advisable to take such intrusions in stride.

On the second lap of the race, Stewart and Gordon became entangled in a pushing and shoving match that eliminated Gordon from contention. Gordon attempted to pass, Stewart fought back, and they streamed into the section of Watkins Glen International known as "the esses" (for obvious reasons) side-by-side, which is not generally advisable. Stewart's car lost traction, slipped into Gordon's car broadside, and Gordon banged hard into the corrugated guardrails. The incident cost Stewart a shot at winning, but he soldiered on to finish a respectable sixth. Gordon's car required some repair, and while he finished on the lead lap, he could do no better than a 23rd-place finish on a track where he had won the previous three races.

Meanwhile, Steve Park, racing on the only Winston Cup track located in his home state, went about the business of winning for the first time in his career. Nostradamus could not have predicted it. Park, a Chevrolet teammate of Dale Earnhardt Jr., had never even finished in the top 10 on a road course. It was his 77th start, and he became the season's third first-time winner, joining Earnhardt Jr. and Matt Kenseth. Park squandered a somewhat comfortable lead near the end but held off Mark Martin's Ford by about five car lengths after the two raced almost bumper-to-bumper in the final two laps.

Despite the exciting finish, the post-race mobs surged as much toward the garage area as toward victory lane. A confrontation of some sort between Gordon and Stewart was widely anticipated, and not without good reason.

Stewart was angry that Gordon, in a prerace conversation, had lectured him on the importance of being patient and then aggressively sidled up to him entering a dangerous part of the racetrack. Gordon felt that Stewart should have backed off and let him go. Backing off, however, is not a part of Stewart's nature. Nor is backing out of a post-race shouting match, so away the two young drivers went.

Stewart used some rather graphic language. Gordon was angry; he threatened to wreck Stewart the next time he got a chance. The show was wildly successful as a box-office attraction. After it was over, a contingent of Earnhardt Jr. crewmen whooped it up and greeted Stewart with high fives and pumping fists a moment after Gordon stomped into his own transporter to regain his composure. Stewart was still bloody angry, of course, but he flashed the trace of a grin before being escorted inside by Greg Zipadelli, PR man Mike Arning, and an extremely frantic-looking Judy Dominick.

"I thought Jeff was going to give me some room, and apparently that was not his understanding," fumed Stewart, still in no frame of mind to address the public.

Gordon came back out of seclusion a few moments later, composed and relaxed. "We got going, and I got a run on Tony," he said. "I told myself that every chance I got to make a clean pass, I was going to take it. I made a clean move, and I don't think he wanted me to pass him. We ran side-by-side in an area you can't run side-by-side. I think he hit the curb and ran me into the wall.

"It's one of those things: two guys going for the same spot. Maybe I was trying to go too hard, too early, but I think there could have been a little more consideration there."

Stewart, who'd been getting plenty of practice in the art of driving through the pack after some form of misfortune, had done rather well in getting all the way back up to the position where he had started. "It's too bad I had the incident . . . because I know I had a great car."

As always after such contretemps, Stewart and Gordon got together the next day and buried the hatchet. While Stewart's temper is famous, no one can cite even one example of his being anything but a consummate professional in putting matters behind him.

"That thing was over the next day," Stewart said later. "What happened at Watkins Glen stayed at Watkins Glen. . . . People who waste their time and spend all their energy worrying about holding grudges from week to week are guys who aren't concentrating on doing their jobs each week. Watkins Glen is behind us.

"There are 34 races. If everyone held a grudge every time something happened, then everyone in this garage would hate one another. When something happens, you talk about it, and then it's done and over with."

26

TONY AND THE PRESS

BROOKLYN, Michigan
August 2000

At the beginning of the 2000 season, Tony Stewart was wildly popular among the journalists who regularly covered the Winston Cup circuit. His extreme candor flew in the face of the less-than-forth-right utterances of drivers who allowed themselves to be restricted on all sides by NASCAR, the ever more paranoid governing body; sponsors and other commercial interests; and their own car owners, who were vitally concerned with those commercial interests.

Stewart's image began deteriorating soon after the season began, though. There was his shoving match in the Daytona International Speedway garage area with fellow driver Robby Gordon, his frequently foul mood after races, and, perhaps overlooked by many, his own sensitivity to criticism.

When Stewart's controversy brought down boos from the crowd, he was hurt, no matter how many times those around him patiently explained that the boos were unavoidable, given his rapid rise to the top ranks of drivers. Each race consists of 43 cars, and each of the drivers has a contingent of fans. By winning three races and setting records for rookie success, Stewart became a considerable obstacle to each of those drivers' chances at victory. In turn, he became a threat to the fans who supported the other drivers. No driver has been booed as roundly in recent years as Jeff Gordon, whose personal bearing is painstakingly inoffensive. No driver has been as successful as Gordon, either.

While Stewart listened patiently to such explanations, he often seemed incapable of coming to grips with the boos. "I can't do that," he said. "It keeps me awake at night. It hurts."

Not enough, however, for him to control his temper. The point at which his image in the media began deteriorating came at Richmond, where Stewart talked candidly with journalists about the increasing strictures on his privacy. A leading weekly publication, *NASCAR Winston Cup Scene*, ran a large story on the difficulty Stewart was experiencing as he tried to cope with his increasing celebrity. Richmond was also the race in which an inadvertent bump on pit road cost him a victory and allowed Dale Earnhardt Jr. to win. Afterward, Stewart was angry and did not try to hide his fury.

Scene was not the only publication to examine Stewart's behavior and interaction with the fans. An Associated Press story by Hank Kurz Jr. examined the topic, as did bylined stories in newspapers in cities as far-flung as Lynchburg and Phoenix. Stewart took the stories personally. He pointed out, quite rightly, that he devoted a considerable amount of time to his fans and declared that the stories were one-sided. Soon it seemed to him that certain reporters, certain broadcasters, no longer deserved his loyalty.

His remarks also caused strain within his team. Joe Gibbs became concerned about the potential effect of Stewart's controversial nature on his image and counseled him to tone down his outspokenness. A hastily arranged press conference was held at Lowe's Motor Speedway in May at which Stewart and Gibbs jointly apologized for Stewart's comments. Stewart also spoke movingly and specifically about his affinity for the fans.

Most journalists still liked Stewart and valued his candor. Some were quite sympathetic when it came to his comments about being smothered by public attention. They had been trying for years to get a driver to go public with such concerns.

During the press conference, Stewart publicly stated that he had not been misquoted, and both he and Gibbs stressed that he'd never meant to insult his fans. Gibbs contrasted the NASCAR scene with the National Football League and said that intimacy between fans and drivers in racing was one of the reasons he decided to give up a career as a football coach for one as a racing team owner.

But the press conference backfired. Journalists thought Stewart was caving to public pressure.

Stewart's increasing isolation from the press hurt him. At Watkins Glen, he publicly engaged in a profanity-laced shouting match with Jeff Gordon. Witnesses conceded both drivers were to blame. Afterward, Gordon retired to his transporter, composed himself, and returned to discuss the matter patiently with reporters. Stewart, however, never reemerged from his transporter. Gibbs arrived on the scene shortly after the incident. Stewart escaped out a side exit, and a handwritten note containing his purported remarks was passed to Pontiac spokesperson Al Larsen and distributed to the media. Whether or not Stewart actually made the remarks was unclear, but they seemed out of character.

What emerged after this incident was a more cautious, somewhat distrustful Stewart. To writers he felt he could trust, he was as open and as intriguing as ever, but he was guarded in the company of those who had alienated him. Perhaps on the enlightened advice of Gibbs and spokesman Mike Arning, Stewart wisely chose not to cut off access to any reporters. What he cut off was some of his personality, at least where certain journalists were involved.

Arning compensated nicely for Stewart's low profile with weekly press releases that could have been used as models within the sport. The releases took the form of interviews, and both the questions and Stewart's responses were topical and lively.

Among the beat reporters, Stewart's popularity was mostly intact. The working relationship had grown more formal, an inevitable consequence of his increasing celebrity, regardless of whether he'd been coached into a more reserved posture. He simply did not have as much time to spend in one-on-one sessions.

Stewart's openness was both his greatest strength and his most serious weakness. It was the characteristic most often cited by his greatest supporters and his most persistent critics. Whether journalists dealt with the brash, opinionated rookie of 1999 or the ever more cautious Stewart of late-summer 2000, he was, is, and probably forever will be good copy.

The success? Well, there was that. However, Stewart's personality augmented the normal volume of column inches and sound bites that would necessarily have flowed from the races he won. Neither Joe Gibbs nor The Home Depot was unmindful of that simple truth.

Or as Judy Dominick, Stewart's long-suffering aide, observed, "You can't help but like that guy. He drives me crazy sometimes, but I put up with it. Everybody does. That's Tony. And Tony is never afraid to be Tony."

27

RETURN TO MICHIGAN

BROOKLYN, Michigan
August 2000

When the teams returned to Michigan Speedway for the Pepsi 400 by Meijer (not to be confused with the Pepsi 400 at Daytona), Tony Stewart was looking for a sweep. Michigan was the largest track at which he had won, and like most drivers, Stewart enjoyed the two-mile track's D shape, moderate banking, and wide surface.

During the week leading up to the race, Stewart had been one of 11 drivers—along with Mike Skinner, Steve Park, Ricky Rudd, Chad Little, Jeff Burton, Bobby Labonte, Jeff Gordon, Dale Earnhardt, Dale Jarrett, and Dave Blaney—summoned to Daytona Beach for experimental tests. Reacting at last to complaints about restrictor-plate races, NASCAR was searching for ways to improve the quality of the spectacle at Daytona and Talladega. The goal was to allow more horsepower (via larger openings in the carburetor restrictor plates), while using higher aerodynamic drag to keep speeds in check. Theoretically, the combination would allow more passing and a better show for the fans.

"We picked a group of guys who are progressive, very innovative, and very smart," said Winston Cup director Gary Nelson.

The tests included height and angle modifications to the spoilers, roof strips, fender-width modifications, and different carburetor plates.

"We needed to do this," said Earnhardt, who had, despite success at Daytona and Talladega, become a persistent critic of restrictor-plate racing. "If we can get the throttle response back, the driver will be able to 'draft back up' [to the car in front], and we'll make a better race out of it."

Stewart, who had found racing at the two tracks maddening, could not have agreed more. He came back from Daytona excited by the prospect of changes and looking forward to the remaining restrictor-plate race in October at Talladega Superspeedway.

"I think the race is going to be exciting," Stewart said. "I think you may see three or four passes on one lap during the race. In effect, what these changes do is allow the cars to create a bigger hole in the air and allow the driver, if he has enough horsepower, to make a run on someone and pass him.

"[During the test] I was leading the pack at one point and dropped back on purpose to see what would happen. Well, I dropped back a little too far and ended up about 200 yards behind the pack, but I was able to catch up to the pack by myself in one lap [Talladega is 2.666 miles around]. That's something that hasn't happened before in restrictor-plate races."

The test also allowed Stewart the chance to spend time with Jeff Gordon and put the embarrassing and costly incident at Watkins Glen behind him.

Dale Earnhardt Jr., slumping since his victory in The Winston, won the pole at 191.149 miles per hour, quite a significant speed since the previous track record, set by Bobby Labonte on June 9, had been 1.266 mph slower.

Stewart arrived at Michigan ranked fifth in the point standings, a substantial improvement since he had been mired outside the top 10 as recently as the end of May. The bad news was that he was 320 points behind the leader, teammate Labonte, and that even while picking up seven positions, he had not narrowed the points gap with Labonte, who had been a model of consistency.

Stewart was not, however, too concerned with his 19th-place starting spot. He had won the June race after starting 28th. "I've just never qualified well at this place, but I always race fairly decent here," Stewart said. "It's just good to get through the first round here [when the top 25 positions, out of 43, are determined], so then we can worry about racing [and not having to qualify again in the final round].

"I'm in a little better mood than I was at this point in the weekend during the spring," he observed. "I guess I just think, well, I started 28th and won last time here. I don't know why I can't qualify well here, but we always have good race cars when we come here. I just don't qualify well. It's just one of those places where, once we get through qualifying, I'm always in a lot better mood after the [Saturday] morning practice and then real good after 'happy hour' [the final session], and then we race well. We'll just see what happens."

What happened is that he did not race well. The bid for a Michigan sweep was over almost before it started.

The race was only 37 laps old when Stewart crashed, and it was his own fault. He had moved up rapidly and was near the front of the pack when he attempted to pass Earnhardt Jr.'s red and-black Chevrolet. Stewart fell victim to a mysterious phenomenon that seems to occur only at the Michigan track. When two cars run side-by-side through the turns, the inside car often experiences a sudden loss of traction. Stewart's Pontiac wobbled alongside Earnhardt Jr. and abruptly skidded out of control.

Who, of all people, was running behind Stewart, minding his own business? It was Jeff Gordon, the driver with whom Stewart had ex-changed bumps at Watkins Glen. Gordon made the split-second deci-sion to avoid Stewart's car by driving up against the wall, figuring the No. 20 car would tend to drift down the banking. It didn't, and Gordon's car became pinned between Stewart's car and the concrete wall.

"I thought [Stewart] was going to save it, but the car 'came around' on him, and there was no place for me to go," said Gordon.

Stewart was disgusted at himself. "I went down into [turn] one, and I hadn't gotten loose there all day," Stewart said. "I don't know why I got loose. It was my fault. I could've won the race."

Unlike Watkins Glen, there was no rancor between Stewart and Gordon, only joint disappointment. The final standings showed Gordon in 36th place and Stewart in 41st. After the race, Stewart had lost 130 more points to his teammate, Labonte, who had finished third. If there was any one week during the season in which even the faintest of hopes at a championship slipped, this was it.

What's more, several press reports, including the lead paragraph of a story distributed by the Associated Press, hyped the crash. Some reporters vaguely noted that Stewart and Gordon had crashed for the second week in a row and chalked it up to a feud, not a coincidence. Despite disavowals on both sides, the actual lead disseminated by AP referred not to the fact that Rusty Wallace had won the race, but rather that the feud between Stewart and Gordon had resulted in another crash.

This misguided hype not only took both drivers by surprise, but it also came as a surprise to many of the beat writers because they were getting calls from their offices complaining that they had not covered "the brawl" between Stewart and Gordon. When they tried to explain that the crash had clearly resulted from accidental contact, editors read verbatim from the contradictory wire reports. Most journalists succeeded in assuring their papers that the reports were, if not wrong, greatly exaggerated, but a few reporters were literally ordered to go back and rewrite stories.

Wallace's victory, by the way, was his third, meaning that he tied Stewart for the distinction of being the circuit's winningest driver to date. The victory was particularly pleasing to Wallace for another reason. While winning poles and leading more laps than anyone else, the Ford driver and former series champion had squandered several races that he likely would have won had not he and his team made strategic errors. This time, when the end of the race arrived, Wallace had four fresh tires, and his chief pursuer, fellow Ford driver Ricky Rudd, had elected to change only two.

Rudd summed up Wallace's victory in seven words: "Four tires, fast race car, short run."

What had sealed Rudd's fate was the "short run." A crash 22 laps from the finish slowed the field at a time when Rudd was comfortably in front. When Wallace moved up behind him during the yellow-flag period, it gave Wallace a chance to use the tire advantage.

"He had four tires, and the rest of us had two, and he kind of whupped up on us," Rudd said. "As the circumstances developed, things played out in a way that put him at an advantage. I don't think I would have done anything differently, but the way it worked out, he had all the advantages when the time came to decide the race."

Wallace figured that pit strategy had cost him three races: one at Martinsville, a second in Richmond, and a third at Pocono.

On the morning of the race, while touring a hospitality tent, Wallace had encountered a rather brazen fan who strode up to him and complained, "You lead all day long, and then you fade back to nothing."

Wallace, a bit stunned, had replied, "Man, that's just not a good way to start the day.

"He was a customer, though, so I had to be nice," Wallace said after winning. "Hopefully, now he's headed home, saying, 'Hey, that's what he [Wallace] is supposed to do.'"

28

LONG, HOT NIGHT

BRISTOL, Tennessee
August 2000

Since 1980, the seating capacity of Bristol Motor Speedway has more than quadrupled. A tiny oval, .533 of a mile around and banked 36 degrees in the turns, is now surrounded by yawning grandstands that seat over 150,000 fans. Even the incredible expansion—the track is tucked in between steep hills—has not kept up with demand for tickets. The second annual Bristol race, run at night, is one of the toughest tickets in all of sports.

The high speeds, high banks, and concrete surface produce a riveting show that is equal parts demolition derby, three-ring circus, and special-effects extravaganza. The huge bowl, decorated in eerie blue lights at night, provides a sharp contrast to the Appalachian mountain country that surrounds it. From the outside, the first impression is that some mammoth alien mothership has landed.

The fans, many of whom camp out for miles around the track, are fiercely partisan but also doting. Driver Robby Gordon, not a household name, told a story that illustrated what makes Bristol a phenomenon.

"The fans at Bristol, and I've only raced there a few times, are awesome, all 7 million of them," Gordon quipped. "I've never seen more people in a smaller place in my life. You can't see the top of the bleachers without binoculars.

"Last time we were here, I went out of the motor-home area after running on Friday, and a fan said he wanted me to sign the tailgate of his truck. I said, 'Sure, where is it? Let's go.' He says, 'No, no, no, hold on.' A minute later, the guy comes over with this tailgate in his hands and a Sharpie [felt-tip pen]."

"That's why I'm here in Winston Cup. Every weekend, I leave with a story about a fan like that, and to start a race at Bristol, with everybody in the stands pumped up, is a great feeling.

Such an atmosphere makes Tony Stewart want desperately, even more than usual, to win a race at Bristol. Stewart, the son of Indiana who grew up worshiping the Indianapolis 500, instinctively values the great stock-car cathedrals. The first race in which he led a significant number of laps was at Bristol, and he arrived at the Goracing.com 500 as the fastest qualifier from the previous year.

"The atmosphere here is unique," Stewart said. "The electricity in the air is mind-boggling. You look up and see all those fans. Except for maybe the morning of the race at Indy, I can't think of anything like it that motivates you to go racing. The atmosphere at Indy is very different, though, but this is probably just as intense."

What evolved on this bright, shining Saturday night was a classic duel between the two drivers who had led more laps than any other drivers during the season: Rusty Wallace and Stewart. Wallace went out Friday night in his blue Ford and won his eighth pole of the season. His lap, at an average speed of 125.477 miles per hour, took 1/1,000th of a second less than Jeff Gordon's. Stewart placed himself comfortably near the front with a lap at 124.930 miles per hour, good for sixth.

Wallace's pit crew consistently got him out of the pits faster than Stewart, and that played a crucial role in his victory. Stewart trailed Wallace at the finish by about five car lengths, officially .501 of a second.

"We had a good car, but we never really got it running the way we wanted it to," Stewart said. "It was one of those days where Rusty really was just a little bit better than us."

Wallace became the first driver to sweep two races at one track and the second driver to win two races in succession, equaling Stewart's feat in June at Dover and Michigan. He also moved ahead of Stewart in victories, four to three. Bristol, however, would mark Wallace's final victory of the season.

"The guys on pit road did the job tonight," said Wallace's crew chief, Robin Pemberton. "It was an all-around good night for us. Rusty did a great job driving the car, and I think we did a good job backing him."

"We were good off the truck [from the moment we arrived]," said Wallace, "and the whole effort was just faultless. Anybody who doesn't believe we've got our act together is crazy. This team is rocking."

Wallace, taking advantage of the pole, ran away from the rest of the field at the outset and led the first 52 of 500 laps, but the middle stages evolved into a battle between Stewart and another Ford driver, Mark Martin, who had started seventh. Gordon, who began the race second, fell a lap behind at lap 314, fading as the engine in his Chevrolet lost power.

Stewart took his orange and white Pontiac to the lead for the first time at lap 147 and, at that point, drove comfortably away from Wallace's Ford. No one challenged Stewart again until lap 270, when Martin slipped past Wallace for second place and passed Stewart to take the lead seven laps later.

Stewart's teammate, Bobby Labonte, took a hit at lap 320. Bobby Hillin, a substitute driver for injured Stacy Compton, spun his Ford between turns three and four, and his car collected another Ford driven by a replacement driver, David Green, who was subbing for Bill Elliott. Behind the accident, Mike Skinner's Chevrolet tapped Labonte's Pontiac, and the points leader lost his place on the lead lap. Labonte wound up finishing 15th.

During the caution period, while workers cleaned up the debris, Wallace was quickest out of the pits, with Martin second and Stewart third. Stewart fell off the pace when green-flag racing resumed at lap 327, dropping to sixth behind Wallace, Martin, Sterling Marlin, Dale Earnhardt, and Steve Park. Trapped outside the lower line—a particularly difficult spot on the slippery concrete—Stewart eventually came back up to speed, but only after dropping three more spots, to ninth.

Subsequent crashes followed in quick succession. Jimmy Spencer and Robert Pressley tangled at lap 343, then Skinner and Ken Schrader made contact at 352. Pressley spun his Ford twice more, the latter time on lap 396 in tandem with Scott Pruett's Ford. Pressley's car practically exploded, but he crawled out of the flaming crash uninjured.

"Everybody up there just knocking everybody else around," said the 41-year-old Pressley. "Just typical Bristol."

During the third of those four yellow-flag periods, Earnhardt's crew made a mistake that dropped him back to 12th place. Earnhardt left the pits third but had to pit again because several lug nuts were not adequately tightened. He never came close to leading again but did manage to work his way back to fourth at the end. At the same time, Stewart, badly in need of track position, took the lead by remaining on the track when the other contenders pitted.

The older tires finally came back to haunt Stewart at lap 410, when

Stewart waves to fans at Bristol Motor Speedway in August 2000. Stewart desperately wanted a victory at the venerable old track, but he came up just short, finishing second to Rusty Wallace.
Tom Whitmore

he was passed first by Wallace and then by Martin. Stewart took second again by beating Wallace to the flag at the next caution, when Ted Musgrave and Dale Earnhardt Jr. tangled.

Stewart never again held the lead, however. With 41 laps to go, Pontiac driver Ward Burton took the lead under caution by having his crew change only two tires (while other contenders were taking four tires and thus having longer pit stops), but Burton's edge was predictably short-lived. Wallace retook the lead almost immediately. Stewart, who had been fourth after the round of pit stops, moved up to second at lap 471, 29 laps shy of the finish. At the time, he was nearly three seconds behind Wallace.

All night, Stewart's car seemed faster than the competition during long runs, (i.e., periods between tire changes). Throughout the season, Stewart had established a pattern of dropping back slightly on fresh tires and then roaring back to the front as he put some laps on the set. Whether because of Stewart's ability to "save" his tires or the setup decisions he made with Greg Zipadelli, Stewart's strength on long runs became a recurring theme of the season. Wallace, in general, performed better on short runs, when frequent caution flags give drivers numerous opportunities to pit for fresh tires. The typical action at wreck-marred Bristol thus favored Wallace and was, in no small part, responsible for his two victories there.

Stewart gradually whittled away at Wallace's lead, reducing it from almost a quarter of a lap to five car lengths at the end. He never threatened to take the lead, however, and would have needed perhaps 10 more laps to make a serious bid.

What probably cost Stewart the race was an incident that had occurred when he was cutting through slower traffic. "I wasn't near as good once I got put in the wall by a lapped car late in the race," Stewart said. "It messed the toe [alignment] up really bad. My steering wheel was probably four inches off, so it hurt the car quite a bit. Right before that, I definitely was a lot faster than Rusty. I just got held up by some lapped cars."

Mike Skinner was a lap down when his Chevrolet bumped Stewart's Pontiac.

"He wasn't the only one [to bump another car], and he was racing guys for position, too, so I'm not blaming him," said Stewart. "That's just part of this track. That's part of this sport, and I had been leading the race and gotten the jump, it would have played into our favor. It's just part of racing.

"I'm really happy with second. I wish I could have caught Rusty, but at the same time, we had a good car all night. The guys kept making adjustments. . . . I was behind the 22 car [Ward Burton], and I think he took two tires [in the pits]. He was racing hard, and Skinner was trying to get by him for some reason. I didn't know what he [Skinner] had to gain, but I could never get by him. He came off turn four and slid up, and in the wall I went."

Stewart's reaction was a far cry from his post-race tirade earlier in the season at Richmond. In that race, he could have won and finished 10th. In this one, he still managed to finish second. It wasn't what he wanted, but it wasn't bad.

"This is my favorite track," Stewart declared later—somewhat of a surprise, given his reverence for Indianapolis. "I've never had any luck here, and this is the closest I've had to having a really good night, and we did have a good night here, finally. But I've always liked this place from day one, and I wish we could race here once a month. It's a great place, and to see all these people here, and the excitement that happens around this racetrack, makes it one of those places I wish we could come to more often."

29

TOO TOUGH TO TAME ... IN THE RAIN

DARLINGTON, South Carolina
September 2000

Darlington Raceway has always required a nickname. Built in 1950, the egg-shaped track was once called "The Granddaddy of Them All," which evolved into "The Lady in Black," which became "The Track Too Tough to Tame." By contrast, it's hard to pin a moniker on glistening, double-decked, antiseptic venues like those in southern California and Texas.

Darlington has little beauty but much charm. It is a glorious anachronism, even with the obligatory high-rise stands that have been constructed to accommodate larger crowds. It is also, by consensus, the sternest test of driving ability on the Winston Cup circuit. The narrowness of the track, unbalanced shape, and abrasiveness of the surface combine to make negotiating 367 laps around Darlington Raceway on Labor Day weekend a testy matter, indeed. The Pepsi Southern 500 is actually 501.322 miles, compared to 400.238 miles for the spring race. The extra 101.084 miles makes a difference.

Driver John Andretti said, "If somebody came up with the idea of building a racetrack today that looked like Darlington, everybody would be up in arms, screaming, 'Why in the world would anyone build a track like that?' The banking on one side is different from the banking on the other. There is pavement on this track that cars have never driven on.

As car owner Joe Gibbs has noted, Tony Stewart "wants to be great." Great drivers win at Darlington. Stewart knew this. Never was Stewart's ambition stronger than during the two-week transition from Bristol to Darlington, a pair of tracks both treacherous and prestigious.

"I know how important the history of the Southern 500 is," Stewart said. "I didn't know when I got down here [began racing in NASCAR], but I've heard the stories, and I've watched the old highlights films. This race is one of the few you can put in the category of races everybody wants to win. It's not the Daytona 500, and it's not the Brickyard 400, but it ranks right up there with the Coca-Cola 600 [at Charlotte]. It's just one of the most important races of the year, and it's one of the toughest places of the year."

The construction of Darlington Raceway, which was built to emulate Indianapolis, gave NASCAR a quantum leap in exposure. The first Southern 500, in 1950, was the ruling body's first opportunity to sanction a race on a paved track. The contest featured 75 starters, and it was won by a Californian, Johnny Mantz, driving an underpowered Plymouth that started the race in 43rd place. It was the only NASCAR race he ever won and one of only 12 in which he ever competed. Mantz was a few weeks shy of his 32nd birthday when he won the first Southern 500, and he was only 54 on October 25, 1972, when he died in a highway crash. Mantz won largely because the stock-car racers of the day didn't have much experience racing on pavement and could not keep tires on their cars. So many tires blew out and went flat that, by race's end, owners were mingling around in the infield and buying sets of tires off spectators' cars.

How the world has changed. Or maybe not. The 51st running of the Southern 500 would not be the most entertaining race in Darlington history, but it may have been the strangest since the long-forgotten Mantz had his 15 minutes of fame.

A 500-mile race victory was still missing from Stewart's scorecard. No one had to tell him that, either. "I'd say it [winning his first 500-miler at Darlington] is a possibility," Stewart said. "It's too hard to predict what the scenarios are going to be and how everything's going to work out, but I hope this is one race that we can win because of history. It's a really important race for me.

"You've got to change your driving style every lap: change where you're lifting [off the throttle], how much you're braking, how much you're on the throttle," Stewart observed. "It changes constantly . . . every lap."

One change would be the tires. In response to almost perpetual complaints about excessive tire wear, Goodyear decided to bring a harder compound to the second Darlington race. These harder tires necessarily led to an accompanying loss in adhesion.

"I think it [a different tire] is going to make the drivers more important, and it's going to make [chassis] setups more important," said Stewart. "The tires do have a little less grip, and I think that was done in an effort to make them 'live' longer. Right now, that's the tire we're running, and we've just got to do what we can to make the thing as consistent and durable as possible.

"We're kind of in a position here where we don't really know how everyone else is going to be when they get here, but it seems like, when we get in a tire-management type situation, we're fairly decent. I'm hoping that will play in our favor. It's one of those tracks that's so hard on tires that, any time you come here, you've got to keep trying some different things that make the tires live longer. I keep learning things every time I come here. I think we learned more this time when we tested. We learned a lot about shocks, and I learned a lot as a driver. . . . Those are all things that will add up and make the team just a little bit better when we prepare for the race."

Neither of the Joe Gibbs Racing drivers fared well in qualifying. Stewart and Bobby Labonte both failed to make the field in the first round. Stewart eventually nailed down the 29th spot, and Labonte took a provisional starting position at 37th. Ford driver Jeremy Mayfield won the pole at 169.444 miles per hour.

Of his qualifying run, Stewart said, "I ran into [turn] one harder than I had all day. The car wiggled a little bit, and it took all through [turns] one and two to get it caught up. That's where we lost our time."

Labonte had a good excuse. He wrecked his primary car in a frightening practice crash and was badly shaken, though uninjured. Labonte had the horrible experience of diving into one of Darlington's tight turns and finding his throttle stuck.

"It was just a freak deal," said the points leader, who did not even have enough time to activate the new kill switch required on the steering wheels since the Irwin fatality. "The throttle did hang on it, and I got in the wall going into turn three. We can't find out why, don't know why, and probably never will know why.

"It was a pretty hard hit. I can tell you it scares the heck out of you when your throttle hangs like that."

To make matters even worse, race day arrived with rain falling and a forecast that called for more. Darlington is not situated in an area known for heavy precipitation, but three of the last four events at the track had been shortened by rain, including the 2000 Southern 500.

It was an exceedingly strange race, marred by one rain delay after another, near total darkness at the finish, and a winner who never led a green-flag lap.

The winner was Bobby Labonte, and his starting position (37th) was the lowest of any Darlington victor since the Mantz upset 50 years earlier. Mayfield led 104 of the first 119 laps but then crashed. Dale Earnhardt was leading, past the halfway point (the point at which a NASCAR race is considered official), when a rainstorm caused a long interruption, but somehow officials got the track dry enough to continue. Only 328 of the scheduled 367 laps were completed.

With black clouds approaching from the southwest and darkness closing in, the pivotal event occurred at lap 321, when a blown engine in Jerry Nadeau's Chevrolet brought out a caution flag. The leaders all pitted, somewhat of a surprise because of the impending rain and darkness, and somehow Labonte, far up pit road from the rest of the contenders, managed to improve his position from fifth to first in the pits. His crew changed four tires in 15.9 seconds.

Only a minute or so later, the bottom fell out on the rain, and with darkness enveloping the grounds, Labonte was declared the winner.

"We didn't have the best race car any part of the day," Labonte admitted, "but we had a top-five car for a little bit of the day."

At various times, segments of the race were dominated by Mayfield, Ward Burton, Jeff Burton, Dale Earnhardt, Dale Earnhardt Jr., Jeff Gordon, and Dale Jarrett. And what of Stewart?

A mistake cost him dearly, but he managed to work his way back into the top 10. At the beginning of the race, Stewart made a spectacular drive through the field from his 29th starting position. He had himself among the top contenders by the 100th lap, and shortly past that milestone, was attempting to track down Jeff Gordon's Chevrolet when his Pontiac slipped into the outside wall between turns three and four. Stewart thought the impact had caused a leak in his right-rear tire. The unscheduled stop caused him to fall a lap down, but when he pitted, his crew discovered that the tire was, in fact, not going flat.

"I made a mistake driving the car," Stewart conceded. "I got into the wall in turns three and four, and then I went down into [turns] one and two about hit it again. I thought I had a tire going down. To be on the conservative side, I came in and pitted and found out the tire was fine. That put me a lap down, but the guys had really good pit stops . . . and I was fortunate enough to get the lap back."

Of Labonte's victory, Gibbs said, "I've never felt so much emotion. That thing must have gone back and forth 10 times. I've never been happier."

The victory was the sixth for the two-car team—three each for Stewart and Labonte—and three of them had been shortened by rain.

Stewart summed up his afternoon by saying, "We had a good day that turned bad that turned good again, so I guess I can be happy with that."

30

RETURN TO RICHMOND

RICHMOND, Virginia
September 2000

Richmond International Raceway had been the site of Tony Stewart's first Winston Cup victory one year earlier. It was also where an accidental bump on pit road had cost him a second victory on May 6. When he returned for the Chevrolet Monte Carlo 400, Stewart had redemption on his mind.

"I think we have proved we can win here if we get the car right," Stewart said. "Being as close to winning as we were in the spring makes me want to go back and kind of finish where we left off, and try to get back the one that got away. The tracks where you run well . . . you always go into them with the anticipation that you're going to win . . . not just trying to run competitively, but to win."

Stewart was not the same angry young man who had flown off the handle at Richmond in April, but he was unusually intense. Rusty Wallace had supplanted him as the circuit's most frequent winner, and Stewart had gone six races without a victory. Mike Arning's weekly press release from the Home Depot team was headlined "Redemption at Richmond."

Jeff Burton won the pole, failing to set a track record with his 125.780 miles per hour lap around the three-quarter-mile, D-shaped layout. Teammate Bobby Labonte took second, but Stewart had to settle for 14th. He expressed little concern, especially after he was lightning-fast in the last practice session before the race.

Stewart took pains to get proper rest before the grueling night race. "Right after the drivers' meeting, I went back to my [motor]coach, took a shower, and basically treated it like after 'happy hour' [the final practice] at a Sunday-afternoon race," he recalled later. "Although I only got to sleep for three hours, it was kind of like what my Saturday evening and Sunday morning would have been like. Then, right before driver introductions, I took a shower, got something to eat, and then went to change into my uniform. I just tried to rest as much as possible and let my body recharge for the race."

Night racing was difficult for Stewart's pit crew. They had no opportunity for a nap. "If it was the first night race at Richmond, at the beginning of the season, it wouldn't have been nearly as bad because, at that point, the season was still new," said mechanic Chris Gillin. "This race is worse because it's so late in the season. By the end of the night, you're worn slap out. When we won last year, by the time one o'clock [a.m.] rolled around, and we finally went home, we were all junk. We were done.

"There's always a chance that you're going to work just as hard as you would at any other race, so you just kind of keep yourself in tune. The more and more you keep your body in shape, the better off you'll be. If you're not at 100 percent, you're done.

"Last year, when we won at Richmond, once we left the track and finally got back to the hotel that night, it was 1:30 a.m. We started that morning at either 7:30 or eight o'clock. We felt the effects of the long day, but because we won, we felt the effects later. When you finally get home on Sunday, and your body says, 'All right, I'm done,' that's when you feel it the most."

The weekend was rife with controversy, and it had nothing at all to do with the race. At the weekly rookie meeting on Friday morning, series director Gary Nelson revealed that a one-inch restrictor plate would be implemented for the following week's race in New Hampshire, the scene of the crashes that had killed Adam Petty and Kenny Irwin earlier in the season.

For many drivers, the very idea of using a restrictor plate on a mile track, one with virtually no banking, was absurd. NASCAR was overreacting to intense criticism from drivers who complained that nothing had been done to cushion the concrete walls at New Hampshire International Speedway in the two months since Irwin's crash. The ruling body had secretly tested so-called "soft walls" during the week before Richmond but had been unimpressed with the results. Despite intense criticism from many drivers, most notably Dale Earnhardt, NASCAR announced the mandated use of plates at New Hampshire to the public on Saturday morning.

"If you can run 'em [restrictor plates] on a flat track, where can't you run 'em?" railed Earnhardt. "This is happening because the drivers are crying so bad. . . . This is happening because of all these whining-ass drivers, talking about how it's an unsafe racetrack."

Stewart privately agreed with Earnhardt, but he held his peace. He had been strongly criticized for speaking out earlier in the year, and he concluded it best to let the veterans like Earnhardt do the talking.

Mark Cronquist, Joe Gibbs Racing's chief engine builder, did speak out, however. He said the changes would require massive reworking of the engines the Stewart and Labonte teams planned to take to New Hampshire.

"It will take all of us—23 of us—working Sunday, Monday, and Tuesday pretty late," Cronquist said. "We'll have guys working Saturday, Sunday, Monday, and Tuesday just to try to get stuff done.

Wednesday morning, we have to load the truck. We usually don't work Saturdays or Sundays, but anybody who's not at the racetrack will be back working."

Cronquist further suggested that the restrictor plates would not solve any perceived safety problem. "I think the stuff they're doing with throttles and brake sensors [NASCAR now required two different kill-switch mechanisms in the driver's compartment, and the Jack Roush organization was producing another device that used sensors to kill the engine when the throttles were wide open at the same time brakes were being applied at full force] need to be looked at more than the motor part of it because, still, the reason they hit the wall is because the throttle stuck, not because they had too much horsepower. The throttle sticking is what makes them hit the wall."

Stewart also pointed out that, with less horsepower, the drivers would be diving deeper into the turns before backing off, meaning that the restrictor plates would allow drivers less reaction time because they would not know a throttle had malfunctioned until even later.

All such entreaties fell on deaf ears, however, the NASCAR brain-trust having already decided on the course of action before opening it to public debate.

"Cutting the motors down is a lot of work for one racetrack for, hopefully, just one year," Cronquist said. "I hope we don't have to keep building the plate motors. If we do that, then we have to start building plate motors everywhere."

Stewart played a role in the Chevrolet 400's outcome, but his Pontiac seemed to peak too soon. Early casualties included Rusty Wallace, usually potent on short tracks; Dale Jarrett, who crashed before the halfway point; and Jeremy Mayfield, who crashed on the front stretch at lap 104.

The middle stages were dominated by Steve Park, the Watkins Glen winner. Stewart tracked down Park near the three-quarter mark (lap 300), but it took a pit stop at lap 297 for Stewart actually to take the lead. On lap 300, Park, obviously faster than Stewart on fresh tires, returned the favor. Jeff Gordon's Chevrolet slipped past Stewart's Pontiac to take second place on lap 206. Gordon's edge was brief, as Stewart's tires seemed to come in, and he reclaimed second at lap 308.

While Gordon and Stewart diced behind him, Park pulled away to a lead of about 3.5 seconds. At lap 316, Wallace's engine, long sour, finally expired, dropping oil down the front stretch. Park maintained his edge through the ensuing pit stop, with Gordon moving up to second, Jeff Burton to third, and Bobby Labonte to fourth. Stewart was fifth when the green flag flew again at lap 323.

This time, Park did not pull away. Burton's Taurus immediately dogged Park's yellow Monte Carlo, passing Park on the back stretch at lap 330. With 50 laps to go, the margin from first to fifth place— Burton, Park, Gordon, Labonte, and Stewart—was only 2.65 seconds.

Another yellow flag waved on lap 353 when Mike Skinner's Chevrolet grazed the wall in turn two. Burton won this exchange of pit stops, but Labonte's crew got him out second, just ahead of Gordon, Park, Earnhardt, Bill Elliott, and Stewart.

Unfortunately, Labonte had to return to the pits a lap later. His Pontiac was leaking power-steering fluid, a problem that had to be corrected with yet another stop in which a belt was cut to prevent further leakage. When green-flag racing resumed at lap 361, Labonte was almost a lap down, just ahead of leaders Burton, Gordon, Park, and Earnhardt. (The NASCAR term for this scoring phenomenon is being on the "tail end of the lead lap.") As a result, Labonte ended up finishing 15th after being lapped by Burton at lap 367.

When one of Burton's teammates, Matt Kenseth, blew an engine at lap 377, Burton's crew ran down to the entrance of pit road to help push Kenseth's Ford off the track, thus keeping the green flag out for Burton. The effort was in vain, however, when the Ford of Casey Atwood, who was making his Cup debut, experienced engine failure at lap 380. Under yellow, the first four drivers—Burton, Gordon, Park, and Stewart—elected not to pit. Earnhardt and Mark Martin were among the drivers who opted for fresh tires.

Gordon, who had started 13th, one position ahead of Stewart, took the lead for the first time on the restart, flashing past Burton with 15 laps to go. He led the rest of the way and finished .744 of a second ahead of a fast-closing Earnhardt, who made use of the fresh tires to move up but could not catch Gordon in time.

Stewart finished sixth, behind Gordon, Earnhardt, Martin, Park, and Jeff Burton.

"If I'd had 10 more laps, I think I could have beaten him," said Earnhardt, who, despite being second in the points standings, had won only once all year. "Park wanted to race me and gave me a hard time getting by, but I got past Burton pretty easily and just ran out of time."

Stewart was bitterly disappointed but composed. "I just couldn't make the car turn all night, especially on stickers [new tires]," he said. "I gave up a straightaway or more to Steve Park in 10 laps on stickers. So . . . it was a long and disappointing night for us. We could never roll the car [apply the throttle] through the middle of the corners like everybody else. The longer the run would go, the better it was, but we kept getting yellow flags after 40 laps. It was pretty disappointing."

He wanted to make it clear that sixth place was not good enough to please him at Richmond, where in the previous two races he had won once and been robbed by fate the other time.

"It's all about winning . . . every week," Stewart said. "You win every week to gain points, so sixth doesn't make us feel any better."

When the checkered flag fell, the controversy did not end. NASCAR officials discovered a problem with the intake manifold on Gordon's engine. It was made of magnesium instead of steel, although supplied by General Motors. The "issue," to use chief operating officer Mike Helton's favored cliché, went unresolved for several days, but Helton said from the outset that whatever infraction had occurred would not be serious enough to overturn Gordon's victory. During the following weeks, Gordon's team received a stiff fine, appealed it, and eventually had its appeal denied.

31

MISERABLE RACING

LOUDON, New Hampshire
September 2000

It was the sad fate of New Hampshire International Speedway to host the two events that featured the low points of the Winston Cup season. In July, on the Friday before the Thatlook.com 300, Kenny Irwin had been killed. In September, when the Winston Cup Series returned, NASCAR made a knee-jerk reaction to Irwin's crash by requiring the use of restrictor plates.

Initially reticent to discuss the use of the plates, Tony Stewart changed his tack when he arrived in New England. His previous caution may have been related to the fact that his Joe Gibbs Racing teammate, Bobby Labonte, had been outspoken in his belief that NASCAR needed to do something to avoid a third tragedy at the track. New Hampshire had also been the site of Adam Petty's death in a Busch Grand National practice crash in May.

On the surface, the Loudon track, slightly over a mile in circumference, had seemed an unlikely venue for tragedy. Since its opening in 1990 and the arrival of Cup races in 1993, the track had never been the scene of a serious injury until 2000. Its owner, Bob Bahre, steadfastly insisted that it was unfair to label his facility unsafe.

Even Labonte mildly criticized the use of restrictor plates once he arrived and took some practice laps. The Winston Cup points leader noted that drivers were so desperate to squeeze speed out of their cars that they were actually going faster through the turns than before. Echoing an observation Stewart had made privately a week earlier, Labonte noted that while the horsepower restrictions slowed the cars on the straights, it enabled drivers to go deeper into the turns before backing off their throttles. Both Petty and Irwin had been killed when their throttles stuck entering turn three.

"I think the speeds are about a second slower," Labonte said, "but I'm driving all the way down to the corner before I let off the gas, so, at some point, you'd have to say that going slower is probably not the right answer."

"It changes everything," added Stewart. "Now the motor guys have to go back and build a special restrictor-plate engine [the one-inch plates were different from those that had been used at Daytona and Talladega]. It's going to make me less comfortable as a driver because, now, I'm going to have to drive in harder [into the turns] than I had to go in before. I'm going to have less time to react if the throttle does stick. It just puts us in a bad spot.

"It's going to make us run slower, but it's also going to make us run harder into the corner because we won't see the straightaway speeds that we're used to. I know that this is all an effort to keep us safer, but now, if we do have a problem where the throttle sticks, we're going to be driving four car lengths deeper into the corner than before. Now we're going to have less time to react and still hit the wall just as hard."

"These are the circumstances we've been dealt," said crew chief Greg Zipadelli. "NASCAR has its reasons for its decisions, and I have mine. Everybody has an opinion. It doesn't mean that I'm right, and they are wrong., or vice versa. It's just frustrating, that's all. We were looking forward to coming back to New Hampshire just like we were the last time we were here.

"When my driver [Stewart] sits there and says this isn't what he wants to do, I mean, he's the man who has to make the call, along with a lot of other drivers who have said this isn't the right thing to do. If Tony told me, 'Yeah, this is a good idea. We'll be all right. I'm comfortable with it,' my opinion would be different. But when my driver doesn't think it's the right thing to do, well, then, obviously, it bothers me."

Stewart would have had mixed emotions, anyway. He'd won the earlier New Hampshire race on July 9, but he'd lost a familiar rival in Irwin. He carefully considered an appropriate way to honor Irwin and decided to wear a helmet identical to the one Irwin had been wearing when he was killed.

"I gave a great deal of thought to it before I went to Kenny's family with the idea," Stewart said. "It is very important to me to preserve Kenny's memory with dignity. I want the helmet to demonstrate the value of his life and to further enhance his legacy. I felt New Hampshire was the proper track to wear a replica of his last Winston Cup helmet."

Why was this an unusual decision on Stewart's part? Because he is superstitious, exceedingly so, and one of his superstitions involved the color green, which had been the most prevalent color in Irwin's helmet. Stewart had worn a green helmet only one time in his career, and on that occasion, he had suffered serious head injuries in an Indy-car race. The injuries had left him inactive and mostly bedridden for three months in late 1996.

The winner of the previous year's DuraLube 300, Joe Nemechek, said, after qualifying, "This is the same as when I used to run Late Model Stocks [at local short tracks]. This is Late Model Stock racing.

We've got 450 horsepower. You can go buy a Late Model Stock engine for $1,800 [it was pointed out later that Nemechek significantly underestimated the cost], and it has that much horsepower. We've got a $70,000 motor making 450 horsepower. They don't run down the straightaway, and you've got to go really fast around the corners. You just don't have any power."

Jeff Gordon was asked how he planned to pass, and his answer proved prophetic. "That I don't know," he said. "Start up front. Passing is going to be a real tricky thing from what I'm seeing so far. I'm hoping an outside groove opens up, but we haven't seen that much here, even in the past."

The race turned out to be a major disappointment, and, for once, the comments made by drivers like Stewart, Labonte, Nemechek, and Dale Earnhardt had not been exaggerations. Labonte qualified first, averaging 127.632 miles per hour as compared to the speed of 132.089 that Rusty Wallace had run in winning the pole in the earlier race. Theoretically, that should have given Labonte a significant edge. The only edge Labonte received, as it turned out, was one that enabled him to finish second.

Stewart, by the way, qualified 16th. "I hate restrictor plates," he said. "Still do. Always have, so there's nothing different this week. Hopefully, we can put on a good show for the fans because it sure feels terrible in the cars."

Alongside Labonte on the front row was Ford driver Jeff Burton, already a three-time winner at the 1.058-mile oval. On the first lap, Burton managed to get past Labonte. With that move, the race was decided.

Burton became the first driver to lead every lap of a NASCAR event on a track longer than one mile since Glenn "Fireball" Roberts had done so in 1961. Not only did Burton lead all 300 laps; Labonte spent 225 of the 300 laps in second place.

In his post-race remarks, even the winner was unenthusiastic about the use of restrictor plates. "This is not the final answer," said Burton. "Maybe slowing the cars down in some other form or fashion is part of an answer. We don't have to go as slow as we did today. We've got to build better walls, build better environments for the drivers to apply things like Jack [Roush, Burton's owner] did with his [throttle] cut-off switch. We have to use the fatalities we had here as a wake-up call."

During the race, though, it was the fans in the grandstands who could have used a wake-up call. Jimmy Spencer, the 15th-place finisher, said it best: "I'm glad I didn't pay 50 bucks to see that show."

Stewart had a maddening array of bad luck, finishing 23rd, three laps off the pace. Poor timing doomed his chances for a decent finish. On three separate occasions, Stewart pitted under green-flag conditions, only to have a caution flag come out either while he was still in the pits or shortly after he had exited. As a result, Stewart lost three laps to Burton and the 10 other drivers who finished on the lead lap.

As a measure of how dramatically the rule change had affected the quality of racing, it was noted that the previous 12 races at the track had featured an average of 14.64 lead changes, and none had had fewer than nine.

"This is not Winston Cup racing," fumed Earnhardt, who finished 12th. "They [NASCAR] just overreacted. . . . It was just sorry racing to me. I hope to hell we don't do it anymore.

"Race cars are race cars, not Late Model Stock cars. They put Late Model Stock cars on short tracks for kids to learn how to race. Here we are, racing the same stuff in Winston Cup, with less horsepower, actually. What can you say? . . . If they want sorry racing for the fans, then that's what they got. If I was a fan, I wouldn't buy a ticket for a restrictor-plate race on a track this short."

"It was real hard to pass," Stewart said after climbing out of his car. He then paused. "No . . . It was impossible to pass. . . . When one guy leads every lap of a race, that should be a good indication of what today was like."

Of course, having driven the race in the green helmet, Stewart could not have been surprised, given his superstitious nature, that events had not gone his way.

Later, an acquaintance of the driver remarked, "If I had been wearing the helmet of a man who had been killed on the very track where he had died, it would have scared me to death."

"I *was* scared to death," Stewart replied. "That whole race, everything that could possibly go wrong did go wrong. I had an awful feeling all race long."

Then why on earth did he choose to do it?

"I just made up my mind that that was what I wanted to do," he said. "I sat down and thought about it, and it was the one thing that I thought was fitting as a tribute to Kenny [Irwin]. Nothing else I could think of was quite appropriate."

32

BETTER THAN BACK TO NORMAL

DOVER, Delaware
September 2000

ompared to the previous two weeks, the second visit to Dover
Downs International Speedway was quite peaceful. Oh, the engines
were roaring, all right, and thanks to the absence of the dreaded
restrictor plates, they were running quite forcefully. The MBNA.com
400 gave the Winston Cup Series an opportunity to get back to normal.

Much of the racing world's attention was focused elsewhere. Indianapolis Motor Speedway, having had a road course constructed to snake
through its mammoth infield, was hosting the first international Grand
Prix held in the United States in nine years.

For obvious reasons, Tony Stewart was happy to get back to Dover.
When he had won there on June 4, it had put an end to his sophomore
jinx. What's more, events since had proved that the Dover victory was
no fluke. Stewart had emerged as a potential winner at tracks of all
shapes and sizes. Dover is where Stewart had begun putting the acri-
mony of the spring behind him. He had learned a few valuable lessons
without sacrificing the essence of his personality. The Stewart who
returned to Dover in September was serene compared to the Stewart
who had won there in June.

Mood aside, Stewart was, however, a bit frantic in his pursuit of another victory. Eight races had passed since his win in New Hampshire; in fact, that track had come and gone again. Stewart had been supplanted by Rusty Wallace as the winner of the most races. He had visited a series of tracks that were his personal favorites—Indianapolis, Michigan, Darlington, Bristol, and New Hampshire—without winning.

The weekend did not begin impressively. Stewart's qualifying run was not fast enough to put him in the top 25 positions. He had to settle for the inside of the 14th row on the starting grid, well behind teammate Bobby Labonte, who was none too pleased with his own 17th-place performance. Ford driver Jeremy Mayfield won the pole at an average speed of 159.872 miles per hour around the high-banked mile.

"It just seems like we can't get it to go around the racetrack," said Stewart after his qualifying attempt. "It's been doing a little bit of everything. That's the thing: We can't make it do one thing. It's tight [difficult to steer] in some places and loose [oversteering] in others."

Stewart had already demonstrated that qualifying meant little in terms of his race-day performance. In the three races he'd won, he had started sixth, 16th, and 28th.

The trend continued. In the Saturday practice sessions, Greg Zipadelli and crew managed to solve the handling problems that had mystified them during time trials. Stewart's frustrations ended once the 400-lap race began. In radio communications with his crew and spotter, Stewart was calm and confident. He never dominated until the final 100 miles, but his frame of mind indicated that he had seen it coming.

Others equaled the speed of Stewart's Pontiac at various times during the afternoon, but only Stewart seemed able to go so fast without wearing out tires. The engine in Mayfield's Ford failed after he'd led 80 of the first 80 laps, but two other contenders, Jeff Burton and Jerry Nadeau, crashed due to apparent tire failure. Burton led 39 laps but crashed at lap 186. Nadeau was supposed to be trying to conserve tires when he crashed at lap 253.

"I just ran too many laps," Nadeau said. "It was my own fault. I was running too hard."

With the three fastest cars conveniently sidelined, Stewart had no real competition. Johnny Benson, in a Pontiac, and Ricky Rudd, in a Ford, offered somewhat tepid opposition during the late stages, but Stewart led by almost a quarter of a lap when the checkered flag fell.

Stewart was almost immediately called upon by reporters to offer some explanation for his success in the race after the poor qualifying performance. More directly, it was pointed out to him that he seemed to race better *when* he qualified poorly.

"There is qualifying, and then there is the race," Stewart said. "Our emphasis is on winning races this year and not on winning poles. The poles are nice, but you get to take pictures with that big trophy when you win on Sunday, not Friday. We're concentrating more on that.

"I didn't dominate all day, by any means. Jeff Burton, Jerry Nadeau, and Jeremy Mayfield: Those are the guys who were really strong all day."

Stewart did dominate when it counted, however. And none of the other drivers had dominated *all day*. Stewart took some time to get to the front, a consequence of his 27th-place starting position.

At one point during the race, Zipadelli had radioed a message to Stewart: "Take it easy."

Stewart's reply? "If I was taking it any easier, the car would fire me."

On another occasion, Zipadelli asked, "How's the car feel, Smoke?"

"Fine, just fine," came Stewart's reply. "Couldn't be better."

"You're down 3.7 seconds."

"No problem. I'll catch them sooner or later. The car is great, guys. Maybe a tad tight, but not enough to be worth mentioning."

With Stewart in that mode, the rest of the field might as well have waved a white flag. Resistance was futile. The overall outcome was also pleasing for Joe Gibbs, whose other car, the Pontiac driven by points leader Bobby Labonte, finished fifth. Stewart and Labonte behaved as if they were jockeys aboard thoroughbreds. Stewart rode the "speed horse" that went out and set such a pace that the other horses broke down. Labonte, meanwhile, closed in on his season championship. His closest pursuers, Dale Earnhardt and Burton, placed 17th and 36th, respectively, and by day's end, Labonte led Earnhardt by 249 points and Burton by 267. Labonte's lead thus swelled by 48 percent in one day.

Stewart rose from seventh to a fifth-place tie with Ricky Rudd in the points standings. He was 459 points behind his teammate. With only seven races remaining, his title hopes were all but nil. He was making a mark, however.

33

HIS FINEST MOMENT

MARTINSVILLE, Virginia
October 2000

The season was beginning to read like an episode of the old television series *Mission Impossible* for Tony Stewart. Every move, on and off the track, seemed fraught with peril, but somehow, Stewart and his team managed to pull off their assignments against long odds.

It was typical of Stewart to say, when asked about Martinsville Speedway, "I hate the place." His next sentence would be, "I love the fans there, though." Of course, the more attention-grabbing part of the comment would invariably be the part that wound up in headlines. It was sort of the same old story of Stewart having his frankness thrown back in his face. Every driver has likes and dislikes, however, and in most instances, his likes coincide with the tracks where he has done well and his dislikes with tracks where engines and tires have frequently blown.

Most drivers do not win at tracks they do not like. Doing so is a triumph over one's own predilections as much as over the offending patch of real estate.

Martinsville Speedway is flat and narrow. From above, the racing surface resembles the outer edges of a paper clip. The rear ends of the cars swing around as drivers attempt to guide them through the turns.

Brakes wear out at an alarming rate. It is virtually impossible to race at the track without occasionally bumping into another car. The track's inner edge contains curbing to separate the pavement from a small patch of freshly mowed grass, and the huge stock cars frequently bound across the curbing, either because the driver slips or because another car bumps or otherwise forces the car down there.

To spectators at Martinsville, though, the track offers a rousing show and no small test of a drivers' ability, patience, and perseverance.

Stewart says he hates the track. What he has perhaps not yet learned is that everyone hates Martinsville Speedway. It makes life difficult for drivers. Eventually, they come to love it. The track was opened in the 1940s, and, like Darlington, it is a much-modernized but still rustic testament to the sport's origins. Stewart cut his teeth in the Midwest, racing on tracks where a race's length was typically 50 laps. A Cup race at Martinsville requires 500 laps of what stock-car fans refer to as "beating and banging."

For all that, it came as no surprise when Stewart won the pole. He already held the track record, set on his first visit in April 1999. He improved upon that with a lap at average speed of 95.371 miles per hour. He had gone on to finish 20th in his debut race at the track, however. Even his qualifying had been erratic: Twice Stewart had won poles, and twice he had taken provisional starting spots. His finishes in his first three races had been 20th, 41st, and sixth. On April 9, he had driven up through the pack from 37th position at the start to earn the sixth-place finish. To Stewart's way of thinking, that seeming achievement had meant nothing.

"I haven't learned anything," Stewart said. "The only thing different about that race was I didn't wreck."

Stewart's pole margin was quite narrow. Rusty Wallace made his run right after Stewart's and took only .007 of a second longer to average 95.338 miles per hour.

"Martinsville is the toughest track I've ever tried to conquer," Stewart said. "I get very impatient here. Usually, my pit crew sneaks in the car and puts a note on the dash about being patient. This time I'm going to tape the thing in there myself.

"This place is one of the toughest to get around. You've got to hit your marks every lap to be good here. The last time I was here, I had a decent practice run, but then, in qualifying, I missed my marks a little bit, and we took a provisional. I'm just glad we didn't get in that situation this week."

Teammate Bobby Labonte, who qualified 14th, also had a rather dismal record at Martinsville, never having finished better than eighth.

Amazingly, Stewart went out on Sunday and won the NAPA Autocare 500, and to do it, he had to keep Dale Earnhardt, a six-time Martinsville winner, at bay for the final 11 laps.

For most of the afternoon, the dominant cars were those driven by Stewart and Jeff Burton, who ended up third. Burton led the most laps, but Stewart disappeared from the front pack for quite some time in the middle stages after electing not to pit for tires when most others did so. Stewart led laps 55–205 but slumped badly, all the way to ninth, when a long period of racing uninterrupted by yellow flags transpired during laps 250–282. When Stewart finally did pit, he lost further track position, and it took him until lap 474 finally to regain the lead.

A late caution period occurred when rookie drivers Dave Blaney and Dale Earnhardt Jr. tangled, thus erasing Stewart's lead and putting the senior Earnhardt squarely behind him for the final 11. Stewart's Pontiac took an ever-so-slight advantage when the green flag waved for the final time, and Earnhardt could never get back to within a car length. Stewart had bested Earnhardt once before, at Michigan, but in that event, Earnhardt's chase had been shortened by six laps due to rain.

Stewart took great pride in holding off Earnhardt, one of two drivers ever to win seven championships.

"It means a lot to me that the race went the distance, and I was able to keep Earnhardt behind me," he said. "It makes you appreciate it more. You know that you earned it.

"We licked the stamp. We sealed the envelope. Throw it in the mail . . . done."

He also took great satisfaction in getting the last word in with a band of his detractors. "There were three guys in the stands over there, at the end of the back stretch," Stewart said. "They were booing me all day, and I just want to thank them for giving me an edge. I really wanted to ruin those guys' day.

"Look down the back stretch," he added, pointing through the press box windows. "The grandstands are right up against the wall. These guys may have been Earnhardt fans. I don't know whose fans they were, but every time I saw those guys—and they were making gestures all day - and every time they did it, I was more determined I was going to run good just to make them mad."

Stewart was almost in a trance. After the conclusion of the post-race press conference, he lingered a while in the wings of the track's new press box, chitchatting with several reporters.

"I still can't believe I won here," he said. "I know it sounds like I'm putting on an act, trying to sound modest, but I *really* can't believe I won. I haven't ever had any illusion that I was any good at this track."

34

LABONTE'S TURN

CONCORD, North Carolina
October 2000

ony Stewart arrived at Lowe's Motor Speedway, a track located right in the middle of stock car racing's heartland, with more victories than any other driver. He had twice won two races in a row and had swept two races at the same track (Dover). The situation could hardly have been more different from May, when the timing of The Winston and the Coca-Cola 600 had coincided with the lowest point of Stewart's season and NASCAR career.

"Everybody just sees that we've won five races in the second half of the season, but the first half really wasn't all that bad," insisted Greg Zipadelli.

Between Martinsville and Charlotte (until 1998, Lowe's Motor Speedway was known as Charlotte Motor Speedway), Stewart reflected on the on-track factors that had made the first 12 races of the season so painful.

"The biggest thing," he said, "is that, with as many changes as we've had this year, there were a lot of weeks that our notes from one race at a track to the next weren't as good. It makes it frustrating for a driver when the car is not driving the same. Greg [Zipadelli] is good at keeping me focused in the car. When he starts hearing that I'm getting frustrated [via radio], he kind of gets into a cheerleader mode at that point. He is able to kind of get me out of that thought process, about how the car doesn't feel good, and gets me concentrating on what I can do to make the car better. We're learning how to play each other's emotions. If I'm on a downswing, he knows how to pick me back up, and if he's on a downswing, I know how to pick him back up. I think that's what we have to learn to do together to be a contender for a championship."

One change that had played havoc with Zipadelli's notes had been the new tire compounds provided by Goodyear. After the season's first Martinsville race, the tire manufacturer had taken away the free rubber it had been supplying to Stewart's team. After his victory in the second Martinsville race, Goodyear officials told Stewart he could get his free tires back in 2001 if he remained on his best behavior for the remainder of 2000. (A single set of tires costs approximately $1,800; a season's worth could easily amount to $500,000.)

The so-called "new generation" tires had been particularly difficult for Stewart in the May Charlotte events. "That was the biggest difference," Stewart said. "It was never that the tires were bad tires. They were great tires; it's just that we weren't able to adjust to them. I struggled to get comfortable on the tire, but it was a better tire for everybody. It just changed our setup in the way I drove.

"I run kind of a unique line here that some of the other drivers don't run," he added. "It affected me a lot more than it affected a lot of the other [drivers], but we ran the [new] tire in the spring and got a little better with it. I'm really looking forward to going back so that we can keep working with the tire a little more. Hopefully, the gains we made from the fall of [1999] to the spring of this year will continue when we get back out on the track, and we'll get back up toward the front at Charlotte, where we need to be."

Stewart then described his "different" line: "It's the same line I run in qualifying. As the tires get older, a lot of drivers will move up off the bottom of the track through turns three and four. I'm able to stay right on the bottom with that setup that we run. It's hard to do that because the track is a lot rougher on the bottom of [turns] three and four, so it's a unique challenge for us to find a balance with the car to make it compatible with the tire."

Once again, the World of Outlaws sprint-car circuit was also running on the Lowe's Motor Speedway property, at the dirt track across the street from the speedway's front straight. Stewart was adamant about attending the races and had worked with aide Judy Dominick to keep his appearance schedule somewhat clear during the time he wanted to spend at the dirt track.

"I'll be what you call a grunt, which is the lowest-paid crew member on the team," Stewart said, laughing. "I don't get paid to go over and work, but I will be helping my friend, Danny Lasoski, over there each night. It's just something I enjoy. With our situation of building a team for Danny next year with myself as car owner, it's really good for me to be seen over there and be a part of it. It also gives me a good opportunity to see what kind of technology there is that I need to concentrate on and what kind of equipment I need to acquire over the winter. We already have a bunch of equipment, and we have a couple of really good sponsors already lined up. It's just a matter of me trying to get a couple of more sponsors and just staying on top of the series and making sure that I'm giving Danny the best equipment that I can give him next year."

Within a month after the Charlotte World of Outlaws races, Stewart and Lasoski would announce a sponsorship from the J.D. Byrider chain of used-car dealerships. Stewart's entrepreneurial efforts in other series were partly altruistic: he wanted to use his name recognition and celebrity to help others who were not making the kind of salaries common in the Winston Cup Series.

"The way I look at it, you can't take all your money with you when you die, anyway," Stewart said. "Trust me: I have a lot of bills to pay each week, but I just really enjoy auto racing. I haven't forgotten where I came from. I haven't forgotten fans who supported me from where I came from. This is a great opportunity for me to help a guy that's in the same situation I was in several years go, before I got my lucky break to the IRL [Indy Racing League] and Winston Cup. It's nice for me to be able to take some of what I've made in Winston Cup and be able to put it in a program to help another driver that I really admire and that I'm really close to by way of friendship.

"It gives me a lot of gratification. I enjoy going racing. Even though I'm not in the driver's seat each night, I really enjoy being a part of that series with Danny, and I'm looking forward to being even more involved next year."

Based on his experiences over the summer, Stewart insisted he was no longer interested in actually driving the winged sprint cars.

"I don't think you'll see me in any competition laps," Stewart said. "I've driven a winged sprint car [Stewart's primary background was driving unwinged sprint cars sanctioned by the United States Auto Club] a couple of times in the last year under aliases so Joe [Gibbs] wouldn't find out, but I've pretty much decided that winged sprint cars are not my bag of tricks. I do a lot better without the wings on top. So . . . I'll leave it to trained professionals. I'll just be the guy who writes the checks and scrapes the mud off the car each night."

Chevrolet driver Jeff Gordon won the pole for the UAW-GM Quality 500, turning his lap an average of 185.561 miles per hour, not fast enough to reach Dale Earnhardt Jr.'s record, 186.034, set on May

24 before the Coca-Cola 600. Bobby Labonte put a Joe Gibbs Pontiac on the front row alongside Gordon, averaging 185.516 miles per hour. Gordon's teammate, Jerry Nadeau, qualified third. Stewart could muster only 183.767 miles per hour out of his Pontiac, qualifying 17th.

On the day before the race, Stewart felt better about changes the team had made. "We're good enough to be competitive," he said. "I don't know whether we're good enough to win it. We can be in the ballpark."

Zipadelli echoed his driver's remarks. "We're not good enough to win right now," he said, "but, hopefully, we'll get where we need to be. We'll just keep plugging away. Is it possible? Sure. I feel that there aren't many racetracks where we can't go and win. I think you kind of have to have that belief in your people and your driver in order to go out and win. We're looking forward to just having a good run."

Unlike the Coca-Cola 600, which had begun at twilight in May, the UAW-GM 500 was run on Sunday afternoon. It was the first time the National Football League's Carolina Panthers had ever held a home game in conflict with a NASCAR race, and the crowd was somewhat disappointing: an estimated 130,000 fans.

Bobby Labonte prevailed at the end of an exciting race that saw the lead change hands 46 times among 13 drivers. Strategy gave Labonte the edge over Ford driver Jeremy Mayfield at the end. Mayfield elected to pit quickly at lap 308 (out of 334) and had his crew change only two tires. Labonte took four in his final pit stop and passed Mayfield with seven laps remaining.

"The last pit stop was really what did it," said Labonte, whose points lead was 252 over Jeff Burton at race's end. "I caught [Mayfield] faster than I thought I would. It was faster than he thought I would, or else, I guess, he wouldn't have changed two tires."

Stewart led 30 laps himself and was actually ahead of his teammate following his final pit stop. The fresh tires did not benefit Stewart, however, who wound up finishing fourth behind Labonte, Mayfield, and Ford driver Ricky Rudd.

"If I would have known the tires were going to be like they were at the end, we would have probably put two on, and that would have freed the car up a little bit," Stewart speculated. "You can hardly tell. They [the tires] all look the same, but they aren't the same."

Prior to the race, a bit of a scare occurred when Goodyear had to replace the tires scheduled for use in the Saturday Busch Grand National event and divert them to the Cup race. The tire giant had had to discard hundreds of tires meant for the Winston Cup race due to a manufacturing defect at the plant in Akron, Ohio. On the Friday morning before the Sunday race, Goodyear had confiscated the right-side tires apportioned for the Busch race and replaced them with a model left over from that division's event at Dover.

Rumors of a tire shortage in the Cup race never materialized, but team members scurried up and down pit road, anyway, buying up tires during the race from teams whose cars had already fallen by the wayside.

Labonte moved to within one victory of his teammate's total by winning for the fourth time. The two representatives of Joe Gibbs' team had combined to win 31 percent of the season's races to that point.

35

AN EXTRAORDINARY SUNDAY

TALLADEGA, Alabama
October 2000

For the Winston 500, the final restrictor-plate race of the season, NASCAR made changes designed to improve the quality of racing without letting speeds get out of hand. Essentially, the ruling body made a tradeoff of sorts: slightly raised horsepower in exchange for slightly reduced aerodynamics.

The aerodynamic changes made the cars look a bit like police cruisers, thanks to a new spoiler attached to the roofs. The rear spoilers were enlarged and equipped with small wickers, or Gurney flaps, and frontal ground clearance was increased. All the changes had the effect of "dirtying up the cars" so that they would punch a larger hole in the air. The idea was to increase the effect of drafting and thus the ease of passing. The four openings in the restrictor plates, placed on the cars' engines between the intake manifolds and carburetors, were increased in size from ⅞ths of an inch to an inch in circumference. The Chevrolet teams were also allowed to use a rear spoiler that was two inches narrower than those on the Fords and Pontiacs.

The goal? Quite simply, more passing.

Tony Stewart, who had participated in the tests at Daytona International Speedway, the circuit's other restrictor-plate track (New Hampshire, notwithstanding), was ecstatic. He had long abhorred the "follow-the-leader racing" that had evolved at Daytona and Talladega.

Despite the changes, what followed was a resumption of the grumbling last seen in New Hampshire, when NASCAR had required one-inch restrictor plates with disastrous effects. This time, though, most teams agreed with the intent of NASCAR's action. Much of the controversy NASCAR brought on itself was the result of a subsequent on-the-fly adjustment.

The teams qualified using one restrictor plate and raced with another. On Friday, Chevrolet driver Joe Nemechek won the pole at a speed of 190.279 miles per hour, the slowest speed to lead qualifiers at Talladega Superspeedway since Dave Marcis qualified at 189.247 miles per hour in 1976. Bill Elliott's Ford was second, at 190.045, followed by the Chevrolets of Dale Earnhardt Jr. (189.391 mph) and Jerry Nadeau (189.947). Stewart put the fastest Pontiac in the field fifth, at 188.827 mph, followed by Bobby Labonte, at 188.738.

So far, so good.

Then, on Saturday morning, when the cars were practicing in the draft (where cars always go faster than while qualifying alone on the track), speeds got too high—above 198 miles per hour—in the minds of NASCAR chief operating officer Mike Helton and his competition guru, Gary Nelson. They decided to change the plates from one inch to $^{15}/_{16}$ths of an inch. The move was comparable to having aluminum bats replaced by wooden ones at the end of batting practice at the College World Series.

Engine technology is a highly variable art, and almost immediately, the change had drastic effects once the drivers practiced with the new plates. The fastest driver in the final practice session, Rusty Wallace, had needed a provisional starting spot to make the field the day before.

Labonte's speed was 36th out of the 43 cars that participated in the session. Marcis, still active at age 59, drove the slowest car on the track; he had qualified ninth.

Dale Earnhardt, the acknowledged master of racing at Talladega, was unhappy with the change but was, by the end of practice, resigned to them. "I don't like it," he said. "It's changing things for one team more than another. I don't know who it favors. They [NASCAR] made the change . . . It's not going to change the drivers going four wide. That's what they were talking about in the meeting [when the change was announced]. They were trying to get the catch-up time and the draft-up time changed, but it's Talladega. You've got to use your head. You've got to race the draft and race the track. . . . It's not going to be any different than it ever was."

Stewart—and almost everyone else at Joe Gibbs Racing—was angry, but once again, he closeted himself in the Home Depot transporter and declined comment. "It doesn't do a bit of good," Stewart said privately. "I can go out and say, word for word, the same things Dale Earnhardt does, and he'll be described as telling it like it is, and I'll be cast in the role of whiner. He'll be telling the truth. I'll be shooting my mouth off."

Labonte's crew chief, Jimmy Makar, immediately requisitioned a truck from the team's Huntersville, North Carolina, shops to bring new engines, tuned differently and slightly reconfigured in the interior, for Labonte and Stewart. When Nelson, the Winston Cup Series Director, caught wind of the shipment, he reportedly tried to prevent teams from bringing any new equipment to the track. When it became apparent that other teams were making the same moves, Nelson let the issue drop.

What followed on Sunday was a fascinating race that, for once, quieted NASCAR's critics. The race had even more lead changes than the previous one at Charlotte. The lead changed hands 49 times, with 21 different drivers taking a turn at the front of the pack. Stewart, in an otherwise frustrating day, led laps three through 12 and laps 94 and 95. He fell victim to an unscheduled pit stop that dropped him a lap behind, however, and had to settle for 27th place.

Earnhardt won for the 10th time at Talladega in what may have been the most memorable of his career. With five laps remaining, the seven-time champion's black Chevrolet was nowhere to be seen amidst the logjam at the front. He was, in fact, riding along in 18th place. Somehow, Earnhardt managed to pass all 17 cars in front of him in just over 13 miles.

"I was very lucky," Earnhardt said. "I kept working the outside, and it didn't work. I got three wide, and it didn't work, so I started working the middle. I knew I had to pass those guys on the inside. I kept moving the middle and kept working it, and finally it started moving, and then Kenny Wallace [who finished second] got behind me, and when he got back there, we started to the front.

"To think anybody could start back in the field with 15 [laps] to go and win this race is beyond me, because, as the day went on, I went back and forth, and nobody had a dominant car that could stay up front if they [the other drivers in the draft] didn't want you to."

Earnhardt's victory was not the only strange occurrence. Veteran Bill Elliott led 40 laps, more than anyone else, and it was the first time in more three years that he had done so. Even Marcis, who had not won a race in 18 years, led at one point. Kenny Wallace, the younger brother of Rusty, finished second but had not previously placed in the top 10 during the entire season. Rookie Mike Bliss finished ninth, only his second appearance in the top 20.

What's more, at the end, Earnhardt prospered at roughly the same rate that Labonte faltered. After dicing for the lead almost all day, Labonte slipped miserably from third to 12th in the final three laps. The misfortune narrowed his still-comfortable points lead to 210.

At the end of the event, as the cars returned to the garage, it was startling to see how many of them had sheet-metal damage: black circles from tires scraping their side panels, crumpled noses, bent fenders, etc. It looked like a field that had just finished racing at Martinsville, and yet the only multi-car crash had occurred after most drivers had crossed the finish line.

A week later, though, Stewart was still sticking to his guns. "I still think they did the wrong thing," he said, in reference to the 11th-hour restrictor-plate change. "The race would have been better if they had left it alone and gone by the results they had gotten from their tests. I don't care who won or what happened. . . . They caved."

36

A RACE TRACK CAN BE SUBTLE

ROCKINGHAM, North Carolina
October 2000

One of the season's highlights for Joe Gibbs Racing had been the DuraLube/Kmart 400 at North Carolina Speedway on February 27. Bobby Labonte had won the race, and Tony Stewart had finished fourth. Stewart had finished better than fourth only once in the season's first 12 races, and he was relieved to be able to boast of significantly better numbers when the circuit returned to the 1.017-mile track in the Sandhills region.

Unfortunately, that old bugaboo, tires, conspired to complicate matters in the autumn race. Goodyear, once again reacting to complaints about tire wear at the abrasive track, brought tires with a harder compound.

"We'll go back to racing, but we'll be starting over," Stewart cautioned, "but springs and shocks [settings] will still be fairly similar. The shock technology keeps getting better every time we go to the track. We did a lot of shock work when we tested [at Rockingham a few weeks prior to the race]. We didn't change a ton of springs, really, but we did try to find out what the new tire would like. We saved a couple of tests for the end of the year [NASCAR allows teams only a total of seven at Cup tracks during the year] just for this type of situation. When [Goodyear] changed the tire for Rockingham, we used one of our tests to try to get a little better handle on the tire before we went back to Rockingham for real.

"The new tire is a little harder and it doesn't have as much grip. It's not as quick at the beginning of a run, but it doesn't fall off as much at the end of a run."

The secret to turning fast laps at Rockingham, Stewart said, is "making sure the car has a really good balance to where you're not having to use the tires by leaning on them hard to go fast. If you can get the car driving well enough that you can run a good pace without pushing the car, then, normally, about halfway through a run, you're really good, and you're really starting to pull away from guys whose cars aren't quite as balanced as yours. They're having to use up their tires a little more than you."

And if the car did not have a balance?

"You just make sure you don't lean on [the tires] any more than you have to. If you have to run hard to keep the pace, then you have to run hard, but you just try to be as easy on them as you can: maybe be smoother on the racetrack by finding a line that's a little less abrasive by changing the balance of the car. There are some spots on the track that'll make your car freer [turn more easily] and some that'll make it tighter [turn harder]. Depending on what your car's balance is doing, you need to move around on the track to help it out."

Stewart arrived at Rockingham ranked sixth in the points standings but in a tight race for the fifth position. He stood 38 points behind Ricky Rudd and 65 ahead of seventh-place Mark Martin.

Jeremy Mayfield won his third pole in a span of eight races, lapping the D-shaped track at an average of 157.342 miles per hour. Rusty Wallace's track record, 158.035 miles per hour, still stood, having been set in February. Labonte qualified second at 157.248 miles per hour. Stewart made the field in the first round but had to settle for 18th. The driver who was fast running out of time in his race for the championship, runner-up Dale Earnhardt, did not make the top 25 and wound up starting 27th in the 43-car field.

On Saturday, Stewart used a metaphor to describe the importance of preserving tires at the track: "Tires are a battery," he said. "If you use too much at any point, they [the tires] never come back. You have to make sure you are not overdriving the car. You've got to do everything you can to make sure you're keeping in the back of your mind that you may have to run on those tires for 60 or 70 laps. You have to adapt your mindset accordingly and not go out and run too hard too quick.

"There are times when you know you are faster than a guy, and you want to move, and you want to try a different spot on the track [to pass him], but you've got to remind yourself to be patient and wait until the tires actually fall off. Don't abuse them while they're still fresh. You have to make sure you don't use your tires up too soon trying to get by a guy.

"It's definitely a driver's game here. The [pit] crews still play just as big a part of it as they normally do, but the driver can really make or break himself. He can have the best car out there, but if he overdrives it in the beginning of each run, he is going to wear [the tires] out Then, guys who may not have as good a car as he has—if they take care of their tires—are going to be better. It definitely puts more of it in the driver's hands."

Stewart's fourth-place finish in February had been preceded by 12th-place finishes in both North Carolina Speedway events during his rookie season.

"We always ran good here in the Busch [Series] car when I ran for Joe [Gibbs, in 1998], and it was a track that I felt I could always have good success at," he said. "It took a little longer than what I thought. Both races last year, we struggled a bit.

"Then, in the spring [actually February 27], we finally got on track and found some things that made the car feel a bit more like the Busch car I had driven here. I don't think it was necessarily a breakthrough race, but it was a race in which we finally felt like we were starting to get close enough to where we could fine-tune and make adjustments to try to get where we needed to be, and concentrate on some areas, and get in that mindset where we were fine-tuning instead of throwing springs at it [using different combinations in a trial-and-error fashion] every run. . . . We feel like we're close enough now that we've got the spring issue pretty much under control. Now we're working a lot with shocks and those things to try to keep the car balanced."

His mediocre qualifying performance did not seem to bother Stewart in the least. "I guess, this year, we've put a lot more emphasis on what we're doing for the race," he said. "Last year, we got in the mindset, at the beginning of the year, that we had to qualify well, just to make the fields. . . . We just kind of stayed in that mindset for the rest of the year.

"The guys and I still want to qualify well, but if we don't have a perfect lap in qualifying, I really don't get too uptight about it anymore because I know how good our race cars are and how good our race setups are. We've won a lot from midway through the pack and back, and I feel like I'm getting the confidence in myself, in the guys, and in the cars they bring to the track, that qualifying really doesn't matter, at least not as it used to, in my mind. There are some places where you do want to qualify up front because of track position, and this and that, but at some of these tracks, it's not as big an issue, and this is one of them."

Sunday belonged to Dale Jarrett, not Stewart, as the reigning Winston Cup champion won for the first time since the Daytona 500. The Ford driver also clinched the Ford points championship with a 2.197-second victory over Jeff Gordon. The victory was particularly satisfying for Jarrett because he had finished second six times without winning in previous races, and because twice he had dominated Rockingham races, only to be passed by Gordon in the late stages.

"No more bridesmaid here," Jarrett said afterward. "I tell you, I was wondering if I'd ever win here."

Two other Ford drivers, Mayfield and Jeff Burton, led more laps than Jarrett, but Mayfield had to nurse his car home with a sick engine and finished six laps behind, and Burton slipped to finish fourth, partially due to a slow pit stop near the end that dropped him from second to fifth.

Stewart never led but had a reasonably rewarding day. At the end, he may have been driving the fastest car on the track, passing 11 cars in the final 35 laps to finish seventh.

Several problems marred the day. His first pit stop was slower than usual because the crew had to remove a wedge wrench (used to adjust weight distribution) left in the car. Later, a loose lug nut on the left-rear tire caused a vibration that necessitated an unscheduled stop.

"Considering the problems we had, I'm not too disappointed," he said. "I don't think the groove I like to run here is the hot ticket anymore. I got to run on top [the outside portion] a lot, and that's where the groove seems to be moving up to. The more I ran up there, the more used to it I got.

"We just keep trying to learn. The next time I come back here, I'll have a lot more confidence about running the top and about adjusting the car to run up there. The car drove good. I just think my driving style, and where I wanted to run on the track, probably hurt us a little bit."

Labonte was fortunate, at least in terms of the points race. After a bit of debris caused his left-rear tire to go flat, the unscheduled pit stop made Labonte fall a lap behind and finish 20th. The potential opportunity for Earnhardt fizzled, however, when his Chevrolet faded inexplicably near the end and finished 17th. With only three races remaining, Labonte's points edge was 201.

"I don't know if I had a bad set of tires, or a mismatched set, or what," Earnhardt said, "but the car just went all to hell. It was pushing so bad, I couldn't turn it."

37

THE COACH

AVONDALE, Arizona
November 2000

L ike many football coaches, Joe Gibbs, for all his relentless enthusiasm and positive attitude, is a natural-born intimidator. He may
even be oblivious to the fact that he can move people to do his
bidding just by looking at them, but the years of coaching have left a
mark on Gibbs, one that is quite functional.

Tony Stewart calls it "that coach's look of his."

Mountains move to please such men as Gibbs, and intimidation is
a substantial reason for his success. In his four trips to the Super Bowl
as coach of the Washington Redskins, Gibbs won three. He coached
Darrell Green, Art Monk, John Riggins, Joe Theismann, Dave Butz,
Charles Mann, Monte Coleman, Dexter Manley, Mark Moseley, and
dozens of other standouts. Three different quarterbacks—Theismann,
Doug Williams, and Mark Rypien—led the Redskins to their Super
Bowl victories. No other coach has won Super Bowls with three different
quarterbacks. Gibbs is a member of the Pro Football Hall of Fame in
Canton, Ohio. Thousands of Redskins fans have told Gibbs they wish
he'd never left. Even today, at age 60, he is sorely missed and fondly
remembered in the District of Columbia.

Since 1993, when he retired from the National Football League,

Gibbs has dedicated his professional life to NASCAR, and it shows. To hear Gibbs tell it, though, he is almost a bystander to his teams' successes.

"Joe doesn't really say all that much," Stewart often says. Joe doesn't have to.

A general rule of thumb in NASCAR is that, whenever someone uses the words "thrilled" or "excited," he usually is not. Gibbs' favorite word is "thrilled." Another is "we."

"We are thrilled at where our race teams are this year."

"We are thrilled to have Tony driving our car."

Somehow, when the words flow from Gibbs' mouth, they ring true.

"I think there are no natural-born winners," Gibbs said. "For me, it has been a lot of hard work in both the sports I have been involved with. I think my feelings toward people may have been on my side. I like people, and I like working with them. In both sports, the key is to pick the right people to work around."

Gibbs learned sound business principles while coaching football. He learned them the hard way. Even as he guided the Redskins to one winning season after another, Gibbs, at one point, found himself in deep financial trouble as a result of personal investments that backfired. He sought out friends who gave him good advice, he kept his eternally upbeat attitude, formulated a plan, went to work, and pulled himself up by the bootstraps. Most of those around him never knew he had fallen into dire financial straits.

Even if coaching had never taught Gibbs the art of hiring quality people and giving them the freedom to do their jobs, he would have learned it in business. Some coaches are martinets, men who keep a finger on every pulse, who charge around on practice fields and in stadiums, roaring at perceived weaknesses and motivating by fear. Gibbs was never one of those types. He met adversity head-on and succeeded by keeping his chin up and working to overcome it. Sometimes he lost, but in the end, not often enough to mention.

One person who had contact with Gibbs in both football and auto racing was Joe Washington. As a 175-pound running back and kick returner, Washington played four seasons under Gibbs with the Redskins and was a member of the coach's first two Super Bowl teams. Washington later participated in NASCAR's Busch Series as a team owner. Since many of the series' races occurred on the same weekend as Cup events, Washington was able to keep tabs on his former coach.

"Playing for an owner like we had at the Washington Redskins [Jack Kent Cooke], Joe learned the importance of giving his team everything it needs to win," said Washington. "Money doesn't guarantee success, but it gives you the opportunity to put your team in a position to win. You have to buy a ticket to get into the game.

"[Gibbs] was going to do whatever it took to validate his decisions on game day. He was always prepared, and I certainly don't remember many times when he was outcoached."

Always, there is that coach's look: that gaze, that intangible something that allows one man to motivate others by the sheer force of his will.

Dozens of highly successful businessmen have entered NASCAR, most believing they could succeed in stock car racing by applying the same principles they had applied in business. Most of them have failed: Felix Sabates, Chuck Rider, Buz McCall, Filbert Martocci, A.J. Dillard, Larry Hedrick, David Blair, Mike Curb, J.D. Stacy, T.W. Taylor, Tim Beverley, Gary Bechtel, and others.

Washington compared football and stock car racing. "This sport is as close to football as you can get," he said. "The crew chief is the coach, the driver is the [quarterback], and the crew is made up of the backs and linemen. It takes everyone playing well to win a championship, and Joe can see that better than some people who have been in NASCAR a lot longer than he has.

"A running back can take the ball, and plant his foot, and make the best move of his career, but if the lineman misses a block, it won't mean a thing. It's the same in NASCAR. It doesn't matter how good the driver is if the equipment is not right, or a tire changer messes up. It's all about working together toward a common goal."

Gibbs has had one winless Winston Cup season, which came when he was still coaching the Redskins. Dale Jarrett drove Gibbs' first car, then a Chevy, in 29 races in 1992. Jarrett failed to win, but he raced to second- and third-place finishes. The following year, Jarrett won the Daytona 500 in Gibbs' No. 18.

When Jarrett left, joining the Robert Yates team in 1995, Gibbs hired Bobby Labonte, who had won none of his first 63 races in the Winston Cup Series. With Gibbs, Labonte has won every year. When Gibbs decided to start a second team, he pursued Tony Stewart with the zeal normally associated with college recruiters hounding high-school blue-chippers.

Stewart still recalls the Gibbs recruiting onslaught with wonder: "A lot of times he'd call me, and the whole time I was talking on the telephone, I was wondering to myself how he managed to find out where I was."

The power of Gibbs' positive thinking is overwhelming. What is also overwhelming is Gibbs' startling lack of pretension. He joyously pokes fun of himself. Whenever one of his success stories comes up— whether it involves a racer like Stewart or a "gridder" like Riggins— Gibbs invariably has a self-deprecating story to tell, usually invoking either his wife, Pat, or one of the sons, J.D. and Coy, who work for him.

"What I liked most about Joe when I played [football] for him was that he respected his players," said Washington. "He respected what we had done to get to that level. He didn't want to have to be a rah-rah type of guy. He wanted a team of self-motivated guys, so he could spend his time making sure we had the absolute best game plan."

Like everyone else, Stewart considers Gibbs a national treasure. Stewart is as motivated as anyone else by the desire to make Gibbs happy. He dreads "that coach's look," but he doesn't get it that often.

Gibbs downplays his own role in the achievements of his team, but he does not understate their difficulty. "If you want to see how hard Winston Cup is," he said, "remember this. We have been doing this for nine years and still haven't won a championship. In the NFL, we won in our second year."

After a suitable pause, he added, "But that is not to say building a winning team in football is easy!"

As it turned out, Gibbs went only eight years in NASCAR without winning a championship. Bobby Labonte was about to give him his first. Gibbs was about to ascend, in NASCAR, to the same throne he once occupied in the NFL.

And it couldn't happen to a nicer guy.

"Joe Gibbs is a gentleman," said Joe Washington, "in the way he runs his business, the way he treats the people around him, and the way he is teaching his boys. He is just a class act. If I was still in my prime as a football player, and Joe Gibbs was coaching somewhere, I know where I would want to play."

38

THE PAST MEANS NOTHING

AVONDALE, Arizona
November 2000

Tony Stewart arrived at the scene of his second 1999 victory, but this time he did not win. Phoenix International Raceway is a mile-long track on which Stewart had won in both open-wheel and stock cars. The track is located in the desert west of Phoenix. A mountain overlooks the third and fourth turns. Almost flat, the turns are banked nine degrees at one end and 11 degrees at the other, and the Winston Cup Series has been holding races there only since 1988. Only the late Davey Allison has ever won there twice.

"Everybody calls it a flat track," said Stewart, "but, to me, one end is flat, and the other end has banking to it. It's a unique place because the radius of the corners is different on each end, the banking of the corners is different on each end, and then you have that neat dogleg on the back stretch, which adds a lot of character to Phoenix."

Stewart said the turns have sweet spots, kind of like the dead spots on some wooden basketball floors, where the ball bounces differently. "You learn about all the bumps and where all the bumps are," he said. "You learn about the spots on the track that have more grip than other spots, or depending on how your car is driving, places where you can go on the track to change the balance of your car."

It is not unusual for November temperatures in Phoenix to reach the 90s, but when teams arrived, it was cool and overcast, with rain forecast for at least part of the weekend.

Stewart struggled right up until the race. He could not get his Pontiac up to speed during qualifying and had to take a provisional starting spot for the fourth time. The other three had been at consecutive races—Texas, Martinsville, and Talladega—during the spring. Rusty Wallace won his ninth and final pole of the season, averaging a record 134.178 miles per hour as Fords driven by Wallace, Jeff Burton, and Robert Pressley captured the first three positions.

"All I know is we're going to have to start way back in the back and go from there," said a terse Stewart.

Predictably, Stewart ran much better in the 500-kilometer, 312-lap race. He charged from 37th at the start to fourth by lap 254. He needed 33 laps to pick up 12 spots, to 25th. By lap 72, Stewart was 15th, and he cracked the top 10 by lap 86. His charge ended with about 40 laps remaining, though, as his car's handling characteristics began to deteriorate. Stewart limped across the finish line 14th.

"We fought hard all day and never gave up," Stewart said. "At the end of the race, the track wasn't in the best condition, and that hurt me. But after the way we were on Friday in qualifying, to run as well as I did for the majority of the race was another example of what the team is capable of. Unfortunately, at the end, the car just wouldn't handle. Then, with the track being the way that it was [oily] after that last wreck, it just didn't work out for us."

Bobby Labonte, who had qualified ninth, fared much better during the race, finishing fifth and leaving Phoenix with a 218-point edge over Dale Earnhardt with only two races remaining.

Jeff Burton, who also had started second when he led every lap in

New Hampshire, won again. In fact, he became the first Phoenix winner ever to start on the front row.

To win, though, Burton had to take advantage of extraordinarily bad luck by another Ford driver, Ricky Rudd, who had a relatively comfortable lead with 18 laps left. Rudd arrived unwittingly at the scene of a crash involving the Pontiacs of Rick Mast and Mike Bliss. Rudd plowed helplessly into Bliss's disabled car, finished 37th instead of first, and fell from fifth to sixth, behind Stewart, in the points standings.

"You pick up the pieces, and you go on," noted Rudd, sadly.

Burton thought he might have won even had Rudd not crashed. "I thought [Jeremy] Mayfield and I had the fastest cars, for sure," Burton said. "I feel bad for Ricky Rudd, though. He looked like he was in good shape. I was going to catch him, but catching him doesn't mean I was going to pass him.

"I was a little bit faster, but that doesn't mean I was going to win."

The victory was Burton's fourth of the season and pulled him to within eight points of Earnhardt, who finished ninth, and second place in the season championship points standings.

39

HOME SWEET HOMESTEAD

HOMESTEAD, Florida
November 2000

Tony Stewart's teammate, Bobby Labonte, arrived in south Florida on the cusp of a Winston Cup championship. Even if the driver closest to him in the points standings, Dale Earnhardt, won the Pennzoil 400 and led more laps than anyone else, Labonte could mathematically clinch the championship before the final race, scheduled for the following week at Atlanta Motor Speedway. Labonte was looking at a landslide victory, a marked contrast to the presidential voting in Florida, which had just been completed, though the results were still under dispute.

The relationship between Stewart and Labonte had grown close during the season. Early on, when Stewart was going through his troubles and lashing out at his critics, there were rumors of some minor discord between the two. It was said that Labonte felt Stewart was more willing to accept help than to give, though Labonte never said so publicly. (Before Stewart began winning races, the atmosphere had been conducive to rumors, many of them unfounded.)

"I *can't* help Bobby as much as he has been able to help me," Stewart said. "I still don't know enough. I don't have the experience that he does.

"He's a great teammate. It's hard to explain . . . how much of a help he is to me and how much of an inspiration he is to me in my career right now. With five races to go in the season, he was still coming up to me after practice, asking me if my car was all right and if I needed anything. Most guys who are trying to win a championship would not be worrying about what their teammate is doing. That just shows what kind of person Bobby Labonte is. He's a great person, and, hopefully, I can be like him one day."

Joe Gibbs compared his drivers this way: "Tony is very emotional, driven to win, explodes, but that is his personality. Over time, he will be able to control that, I hope. Bobby is more reserved and controlled, but Bobby will go off sometimes. He has it in him."

Labonte carefully chooses his words. At times, he can be hard to decipher. He has a habit sometimes of contradicting himself within the space of a few words, but he was clear in explaining his relationship with his teammate. "Over the past couple of years, since Tony came on with Joe Gibbs Racing, it excelled our team from, like, a sixth-place [in points] to a second-place car [Labonte's points finish in 1999]," Labonte said. "I know we sometimes go down different paths, but we usually reach the same one by the end of the day. We nitpick and try to find out what might be better at certain times, and I think that's helped both of us out and made us better. There is no doubt that the stability of our team has helped the 20 car out as far as going from their rookie season to this year's sophomore season. We gave them stability in finishing races and being competitive. There's also no doubt that we've helped each other out and that it's been a great experience."

Homestead-Miami Speedway had joined the circuit in 1999, and Stewart and Labonte had finished first and second, respectively, in the only previous race. Labonte made no secret of his desire to get the championship wrapped up.

"The sooner, the better," Labonte said. "Inside the race team, [clinching the championship at Homestead] is what we want to do. We want to do it as soon as we can, just for the fact that it would be fun. I'm 200 [actually 218] points up this year and was 200 points behind last year, about a 400-point swing. It's really just no different, except for maybe a few things we learned last year that have helped us this year. Our team is the same. The guys working hard are the same. The mistakes that we made together last year, we just haven't made this year."

Steve Park, the last driver to make a qualifying run, won the pole, ousting Ricky Rudd's Ford with a record lap at a 156.440 mile-per-hour average speed. Rudd's speed was 156.408 miles per hour, followed by Labonte (156.223 mph) and Jimmy Spencer (156.191). All four broke the previous record.

Stewart qualified 13th, but afterward, he said, "I've got a lot better car than my qualifying performance shows."

By race day, it was Stewart who was considered the favorite, and he did not disappoint. In the final practice session, his best lap was .213 of a second faster than anyone else's.

Even during Gibbs's illustrious football career, he never won two Super Bowls in one day. Stewart and Labonte presented the ex-coach with a doubleheader sweep. Stewart won for the sixth time, clinching the distinction as the season's leader in victories, and Labonte wrapped up the championship. Neither achievement was closely contested.

Stewart led 166 out of 267 laps around the 1.5-mile oval, remaining the only driver to win a Cup race at the track. The No. 20 Pontiac, outfitted with a special paint scheme, steamed into the lead on the 53rd lap and led all but 48 of the 214 afterward.

Labonte, driving Gibbs's other Pontiac, finished fourth behind

Stewart, Jeremy Mayfield, and Mark Martin. His closest pursuers in the points chase, Jeff Burton and Dale Earnhardt, finished 11th and 20th, respectively.

"I knew I had a car that was definitely strong," Stewart said. "Normally, and traditionally, our car comes out really strong in the beginning of a run, but I was able to keep that up the whole race. . . . I just had to take care of it all day and make sure I didn't do anything to put myself in jeopardy."

What put Stewart in jeopardy was the heat. Unlike Phoenix, temperatures were tropical at the track, which is located between the Everglades and the Florida Keys, about a half-hour drive south of Miami. Stewart has occasional bouts of claustrophobia, and heat fatigue aggravates the problem. Fortunately, Greg Zipadelli has become an experienced hand in dealing with the condition.

At about lap 130, Stewart reported that he was struggling. During his next pit stop, while the car was being serviced, Stewart opened the front of his uniform while crewman poured a bag of ice chunks onto his chest. By lap 180, Stewart radioed that he was feeling better, and four laps later, he passed Rudd to take the lead for 27 laps. He relinquished the lead briefly due to another pit stop on lap 211. He retook the lead eight laps later and, from that point on, gradually distanced himself from the remainder of the field, crossing the finish line 4.561 seconds ahead of Mayfield.

"Tony was in a class by himself," said Park, the eighth-place finisher.

"I didn't have anything for him," added Rudd. "He was just playing with us all day."

Stewart, who in 1999 had been the first rookie in modern history to win as many as three races, set another, somewhat obscure record by breaking Earnhardt's 1980 mark of five victories in a sophomore season.

"I think the beginning of the race made me feel good because, last year, it took me a long time to get to the front," Stewart said. "[In 1999] it seemed like guys were pulling out big leads on me, kind of like what we did this time. With this track being so flat and with the corners being so big, along with everybody doing such a good job developing their aerodynamic packages, the field tends to separate a lot here. It's hard to stay at the bottom of the racetrack [in the turns], but if you can stay on the bottom of the track, you'll have days like we did today.

"We obviously wanted to finish higher in the points than we did last year [fourth], but if we couldn't do that, then we wanted to win more races, which we did: We doubled it from last year. It's awesome, and a lot of the reason for it is Greg Zipadelli. He becomes a better crew chief every week, and the cars get better, too. I'm still learning, as well. If we can continue to grow together like this, I think some great things can happen in the future."

After the race, winner Stewart and points champion Labonte toured the track in their Pontiacs, side by side, waving to the crowd. It was a memorable moment, compared by some observers to the season finale of 1996, when Labonte had won at Atlanta on the same day that his brother, Terry, wrapped up the championship.

"What most people don't realize and might not understand is that we're going to be celebrating [Labonte's] championship right beside his guys," said Stewart. "It's not like they're going to be celebrating, and we're not. We're all one race team. We all are part of that championship, just like Bobby is a part of our six wins. That just how we tailored our teams. Bobby is a phone call away. When we get back [to the headquarters in Huntersville, North Carolina], we will all be there celebrating because we're a team."

Such a scene could not have been more pleasing to Gibbs, the coach of champions and preacher of unity.

"Joe sets the standard for everything," Stewart said simply.

40

THE FAMOUS FINAL SCENE

HAMPTON, Georgia
November 2000

The Winston Cup season's final race was an anticlimax, nowhere more so than at Joe Gibbs Racing. The teams of Tony Stewart and Bobby Labonte trudged off to Atlanta Motor Speedway, but Labonte had already clinched his championship, and Stewart had clinched the distinction of winning the most races. In a sense, the pressure was gone, so both teams went off with nothing to lose and something, but certainly not everything, to gain.

Stewart now had time to digest the events of the season. He had known both ordeal and triumph. What pleased him most was the realization that his friends had stuck with him through it all. From Jeff Patterson, the man who doubled as gas man on his pit crew and driver of his motor coach (known to almost everyone as "Gooch") to Cary Agajanian, his combination lawyer-agent, Stewart had been well represented by those around him.

With Stewart, it is not an entourage; it is a family. His mother, Pam Boas, literally runs the Tony Stewart business empire. She and his father, Nelson Stewart, divorced when Tony was in high school, but he has never lost touch or had overly strained relations with either.

"My whole family has always supported me," Stewart said. "Mom was a little more reserved and a little more quiet about it than my father was. My father was kind of the ringleader. He was the one who made all the decisions on what we did and didn't do. While she was a little bit reserved, she was, and is, one of my biggest supporters.

"She basically runs the whole office. She does the merchandising, handles my personal sponsorships, pays the bills, makes sure I get to and from where I need to be . . . just all the business that I conduct, she oversees all of it.

"So far, it works really well. Instead of ordering me around like she used to when I was little, now I get to order her around," Stewart said, laughing. "She does a really good job for me. A lot of people warn you about having your family work in your business, but it's probably the best thing I've ever done as far as my business is concerned. I've even got my sister [Natalie] helping me. It's given me the ability to focus on my racing with Home Depot and not worry so much about what's going on with my business."

On the road, Judy Kouba Dominick handles many of the same duties as Boas, and it would not be inaccurate to describe her as a second mom. She probably feels Tony Stewart's pain more than he does.

Agajanian, who is often at the track because he co-owns a Busch Series team, is the son of one of the greatest promoters in the history of American motorsports, the late J.C. Agajanian. Stewart would probably be uncomfortable with a lawyer who did not share his understanding of motorsports.

"I was in racing a long time before I was in law," Agajanian said.

Another *ex officio* member of the Stewart family is Bob Burris, the supremely loyal pilot responsible for flying Stewart and his colleagues from place to place, often on short notice.

Jeff "Gooch" Patterson had once been Stewart's roommate for three and a half years. Patterson said he worked for and with Stewart "because I know Tony and his team are going to win a lot of races and championships, and there's nobody else out there I'd put that much stock in. I mean, I could be staying at home every week. If I weren't working for Tony, I probably wouldn't be out there."

Stewart could not be the racing whirlwind he is without a coterie of associates he can trust. He is involved in the Indy Racing League as part owner of a team, started his own World of Outlaws sprint-car team for friend and driver Danny Lasoski, races his own dirt late model when his schedule allows, and occasionally takes up local promoters on offers to race at their tracks. As amazing as this may sound, he even owns a team of greyhounds that have raced profitably throughout Florida for the past two years.

Within the Home Depot team, Stewart has benefited greatly from the public-relations savvy of Mike Arning, and it is not uncommon to find virtually the entire team off with Stewart on some adventure: go-kart racing, bowling, trips to sprint-car races, etc. Greg Zipadelli and Stewart fish together when time allows, and the "car chief," Scott Diehl, has often tagged along to assist Stewart with his dirt car. What Stewart had around him all year was a group knit so tight that controversy and adversity could not pull it apart.

Stewart had never expected to achieve so much in as short a span as two seasons. Like most great talents, he is modest and unimpressed with his own abilities. He does not understand why they seem so spectacular to others who do not share his natural ability.

"I was going to be happy just being a part of Winston Cup racing," Stewart said. "To be able to win nine races in two years so far, and to be able to do what I've done in such a short period of time . . . I'm just very excited about what the future holds for me. I feel like I've hit the lottery with this team. Not many people in this garage area have had the opportunities that we've had. We still have to go out and do our jobs each week, but we've been able to get all the tools that not only allow us to do our job but allow us to do our job well."

So what was next? A championship of their own?

"Last year," said Zipadelli, "we said we had to grow in some areas. This year, we'll look back on the season and say we have to grow in some areas to be a championship contender. Our [inconsistency] is what has hurt us. We haven't had many boring days this year. We're always battling back from something. I think that shows the strength of this team, which is a very positive thing to have. There are a lot of teams that have bad days and don't battle back, or can't battle back, or give up. If you go back through this year and last year, and look to see how many times we were one or more laps down and wound up finishing in the top five, it would be impressive. Those are the things that are going to make us a championship contender down the road.

"What we have to do is not have any DNF's ["did not finish"] next year. . . . If you give us every one of those races where we were running in the top five before we had trouble, if we could have those back, we'd have been a threat this year. Our goal is to win as many races as we can and, obviously, to finish as high as we can in the points and contend for a championship. Next year, maybe we will be [champions]. Next year at this time, maybe we'll be sitting here again saying we still need to mature and grow in certain areas. But as long as we're winning races, and we're competitive week-in and week-out, then it's easier to look, and grow, and be excited about things. We're fortunate enough to have been able to win six races this year. We probably had chances at five or seven other ones that we weren't able to capitalize on. That's pretty exciting."

At Atlanta Motor Speedway, they had one race to go, and it extended the season by one day. For some reason, the Atlanta area habitually metamorphoses into something akin to Montana, weatherwise, when NASCAR comes to town, and the NAPA 500 was postponed until Monday, November 20, after rains fell all day on Sunday.

Jeff Gordon started out front, having qualified at 194.274 miles per hour, and his Hendrick Motorsports teammate, Jerry Nadeau, started alongside in another Chevrolet. The qualifying efforts of the two Gibbs Pontiacs were typical: Bobby Labonte qualified ninth, while Stewart was 17th.

The season had one more surprise in it. Nadeau, a friend of Stewart's, won for the first time. He shot past Pontiac driver Ward Burton on a restart with seven laps remaining to become the fourth first-time winner of 2000. Dale Earnhardt Jr., Matt Kenseth, and Steve Park had produced first-time victories earlier in the year.

"You couldn't have written this any better," said Nadeau, 30, who held off Dale Earnhardt after disposing of Burton.

Labonte finished a rock-solid fifth, but Earnhardt's second-place finish in the race enabled him to slip past Jeff Burton, Ward's younger brother, to take second in the final points standings.

Another driver who lost a position in the points was Stewart, the victim of a crash in turn two on the 110th of 325 laps. Stewart radioed the crew that the car was loose entering the turns and tight from the center of the corners through the exit. Three laps later, the right-front tire blew, and the orange-and-white Pontiac shot into the wall, flattening its right side.

The whole set of circumstances seemed strange, and when Stewart returned to the garage from a mandatory visit to the infield hospital, he learned why. "Greg [Zipadelli] said we made a mistake," Stewart said. "Somehow, when the tire carriers brought the tires over the [pit] wall [during a pit stop], the right-front tire got put on the left front, and the left-front got put on the right front. I knew the set of tires didn't feel as good as the last set did. Now I know why."

It was a sheepish end to a glorious season, and Stewart placed 38th out of 43 cars. Though Ricky Rudd also had problems and finished 24th, four laps off the pace, he gained enough points to drop Stewart from fifth to sixth in the final standings.

"Oh, well," said Stewart. "There's nothing I can do about it. It's over."

It was, however, fitting that the end of the Winston Cup season did not signal the end of Tony Stewart's visits to victory lane. On Thanksgiving night, at Irwindale Speedway in the Los Angeles area, Stewart climbed into a Midget car and won the 60th running of what is known as the annual Turkey Night Grand Prix.

It marked the 25th victory of Stewart's career in Midget competition sanctioned by the United States Auto Club. He was the national champion in both 1994 and 1995.

"When you run Midgets, there are a lot of marquee events," Stewart said. "The Chili Bowl in Tulsa, the Night Before the 500 at Indianapolis Raceway Park, the Hoosier [now RCA] Dome [race], and Turkey Night's on that list. It's a little more special for me because my longtime friend, attorney, and business manager, Cary Agajanian, along with his family, has promoted the event for years. It's an important race for me because of his involvement and his family's involvement in the past. The race has a lot of history behind it, and it's just a marquee event for Midget racing."

Stewart drove a car owned by Steve Lewis, with whom he had been when he won the 1995 national championship. "I think Joe [Gibbs] understands this is relaxation for me," Stewart said. "I think he's realizing that this is what I have to do to reset myself over the wintertime. It makes me feel more ready when I climb into the Home Depot Pontiac for [General Motors] testing down at Daytona in January. It's nice that Turkey Night comes at the end of the year, the week after we finish our Winston Cup schedule. It's good for me to be able to go out there the next week and know that I'm still sharp from running the weekend before. It's an excellent way to start my offseason."

What offseason?

Stewart competed in the 100-lap event for the second consecutive year. In 1999, he had dominated the race until an oil-pump belt broke on his car with two laps to go.

This time, Stewart qualified sixth out of 56 cars but started on the pole because the first six qualifiers were inverted (typical in open-wheel short-track events). The driver of Steve Lewis's second car, Kasey Kahne, took the lead at the halfway point, but Stewart regained control of the final 25 laps.

"I have been waiting 364 days for this," said Stewart, noting his setback the year before. "Losing last year has bothered me ever since that night. I really had to work harder than I do in some Winston Cup races."

For the product of the Indiana short tracks, it was just like old times.

Index

The Author

M onte Dutton is the motorsports writer at the *Gaston Gazette* in Gastonia, North Carolina. Dutton's work appears in "NASCAR This Week," a page that appears in more than 500 newspapers across the United States. He also writes a weekly column, "Monte Dutton on NASCAR." Both are syndicated by Universal Press Syndicate of Kansas City, Missouri. The author also works as Winston Cup Correspondent for the weekly trade papers *FasTrack*, of Gastonia, North Carolina, and *Area Auto Racing News*, of Trenton, New Jersey, and for the GoCarolinas and RacingOne web sites. His work has appeared in a number of magazines, including *Details, Heartland USA, Racing Milestones, Winston Cup Illustrated*, and *Inside NASCAR*. He is the winner of the Eastern Motorsports Press Association's Writer-of-the-year award for 1999. Monte Dutton is a graduate of Furman University (class of 1980) and lives in Clinton, South Carolina.